Jchn Sadoc Smiley

History of Tennessee River Baptist Association

North Carolina, from the year 1830 to the year 1892 - introduced by early sketches of the Baptist Church, closing w th twenty-four life sketches and a miscellaneous supplement

John Sadoc Smiley

History of Tennessee River Baptist Association
North Carolina, from the year 1830 to the year 1892 - introduced by early sketches of the Baptist Church, closing with twenty-four life sketches and a miscellaneous supplement

ISBN/EAN: 9783337302207

Printed in Europe, USA, Canada, Australia, Japan

Cover: Foto ©Lupo / pixelio.de

More available books at **www.hansebooks.com**

HISTORY

OF

Tennessee River Baptist Association,

NORTH CAROLINA.

FROM THE YEAR 1830 TO THE YEAR 1892.

Introduced by Early Sketches

OF

THE BAPTIST CHURCH,

Closing with

TWENTY-FOUR LIFE SKETCHES

AND A

MISCELLANEOUS SUPPLEMENT

All BY

ELDER JNO. S. SMILEY.

BRYSON CITY, N. C.:
"TIMES" JOB PRINT.
1893.

CONTENTS.

Preface.

After sixteen years from the time the Author commenced to collect material for this work, he has finally succeeded in producing the present volume, which he sincerely submits to the churches and people of Tennessee River Baptist Association, and all other friends of the Baptist Church for their patronage and careful reading. He has given what he thought to be of greatest interest and value to the reader, and has labored with an eye to the welfare of future generations.

We are confident that the facts set forth, lines traced, etc., are a historical legacy not to be ashamed of.

The work has been arranged so as to give the origin of the Baptist Church and its tenets, which distinguish Baptists from all other denominations.

Beginning with the preaching of John the Baptist, we have introduced some leading features and history of the Baptists, following from the early age to the first churches and Associations in America, without giving a full detail of such early history, that we might link the chain of facts and doctrine of the present with the past and thus show how Tennessee River churches and the other Associations and churches of Western North Carolina and America came into being upon the principles laid by the "FOUNDATION STONE."

The origin of the Philadelphia Association and the first churches composing it are given, as it was the first Association in America. From Philadelphia came brethren to North Carolina and established Sandy Creek Association, the origin of which is shown in this work; and from Sandy Creek to Holston Association, and from Holston and Broad River Associations came French Broad Association, the first Association in Western North Carolina west of the Blue Ridge. Then coming westward our mother, Tuckaseige Association, is noticed, to which we find linked the Tennessee River, under the organized name of Friendship, at first, and still further on by the name, Valley River, until 1880, when the present name was given.

The narrative of Tennessee River history from organic period, 1861 to 1892, is divided into thirteen chapters, in which will be found very interesting facts of history and statistics: valuable Historical Tables at the close.

There are over twenty biographies given under the head, "LIFE SKETCHES," whose work as ministers of Jesus, when we consider their opportunities, will, we think, equal anything in modern biography.

To the work there is added a Miscellaneous Supplement, containing Baptist

Marks, What constitutes a church, Baptist Associations—What they are, Deliberative Assembly Guide and other useful matter, all of the first importance as a book of use and reference to all classes of people.

The Deliberative Assembly Guide will meet the wants of Mass meetings, Societies, Churches, Associations, Conventions, Legislative bodies, etc., for it is Parliamentary Law all in a nutshell.

The book is not whollly local to Tennessee River Association, but is well adapted to general use for good, in all sections and among all classes.

The author now puts his humble efforts into the merciful hands of a generous public.

JNO. S. SMILEY,
Swain, N. C.

Feb. 7, 1893.

CHAPTER I.

INTRODUCTION.

The foundation work of the church commenced with the preaching of John the Baptist in the wilderness of Judea, and the first converts of whom the church at Jerusalem was built and from whom Jesus doubtless selected his apostles, were baptized in the Jordan, (Math. 3rd chapter and John 1; 35 to 50.) Evangelism and the true model of baptism, such as was heaven approved, was commenced by John the Baptist.

Certainly the manner in which our Lord and Saviour received baptism at the hands of his forerunner, is that manner in which his true followers were to receive it in the succeeding days of the gospel period. This, we hope, will answer the question, "When did the Baptist church originate?"

The first local church organized was at Jerusalem about the year 31. and the spread of the gospel to the Gentiles and their admission to the church was in the year 41. So, of the early church among both Jews and Gentiles, the reader is referred to the acts of the Apostles, the various epistles and the Revelations, for the local names of churches, officers and ordinances. From the the New Testament containing the examples of Christ and the apostles do the christians known as Baptists receive their true knowledge of church work, discipline, faith and practice.

The first century of Christianity had the benefit of the apostles, as we are informed in case of John, until A. D. 100, by whom the New Testament was written, and by whose inspired examples under the immediate presence and teachings of Christ true church law was given. Confession of sins or fruits mete for repentence and baptism by immersion upon a profession of the the individual's faith in Christ, is the acknowledged way in which members were received into the church by the Apostles of old, and to this the true Baptists of the many centuries that have passed since, have adhered

One of the grossest errors of the early times was the baptism of unconcious infants. This was commenced in Africa about the year 250. With this error came the idea of baptismal regeneration, which is no where sustained by Paul, Peter, John, or any of the inspired writers. Another grave error was the institution of clinic baptism, or sprinkling or pouring for baptism instead of immersion, the first recorded instance of which was performed in case of Novation of Rome on account of his sickness, which made it impossible to immerse him, as they thought.

Uniting State and Church in the time of Constantine and giving to the Civil Magistrates control in matters of religion and conscience, was another error more malignant than any we have enumerated because it gave it to the Bishop and the Emperor, under sanction of law, the right to enforce the forms and rites of religion prescribed in the liturgy by severe penalties, inflicting death to those who dissented.

HOW TO FIND THE TRUE CHURCH.

A wise writer has said that to find the true church in those corrupt times is to look for it outside of the so-called church. The usurpation of the Orthodox, as those so-called churches, were termed by their ecclesiastical historians, whose bishops invoked imperial authority to enforce their dogmas, were seceded from by those who held to scriptural authority. Those who dissented from the Catholics in doctrine and practice were found all along, but we must remember that they have not been called Baptists every time. Adherents of gospel truth of the ages down to the reformation, being denominated "Heretics" or otherwise.

Again, we must remember that we find the true Baptists denominated by the names of certain noted men or leaders among them in different countries and at different periods,—which names were assigned them by their adversaries.

But let Baptists appear under whatever name they may, in any period of time, and in any country, their doctrine and sufferings for Christ's sake identify them well

We find a peculiar people, all a long, who would not baptise infants nor recognise the baptism of the semi-pagan semi-christian and philosophic State church sanctioned and decreed by Constantine and Justinian laws. Examine the New Testament and true church hisory, and when you find a people who baptised by immersion, resisted the uniting of State and Church, and a people who never used any secular power to disciple the people, but instead preached and practiced a pure gospel to the people and relied on the spirit of God to guide men to duty, and you find Baptists in the true sense. Baptists have also been strict in Baptism, believing that none have a right to the Lord's table but such as have been baptised by immersion upon a profession of faith. Another burning feature by which to track the Baptists is by the blood of their martyrs. They would not shed blood to propagate their faith, but their blood has often been shed to make them conform to state religions.

Even after the reformation when it was expected that christians should be free in matters of religion, the poor Baptists suffered much by those who should have been their friends.

State Church under Protestant was as dictatorial and cruel when it interfered in religion, prescribing modes of worship, as that of the Catholic.

But printing gives rapid strides to truth and the dark clouds and bloody days of persecution must go.

The wilderness of America during the seventeenth century becomes an asylum for the church, but even here Baptists are visited by fines and imprisonments.

CHAPTER II.

AMERICAN CHURCHES AND ASSOCIATIONS.

We omitted following, in detail, the names of the churches and noted preachers in the Old World in order to abridge this work, but will now take up a few names of the American beginnings in detail.

The first church formed in Deleware was Welch Tract, with sixteen members, all Baptists, who emigrated in a body from Wales in 1701 Thomas Griffeth, one of these emigrants, became pastor of this church The first church in Massachusetts was Swansea, organized in 1663. The first church formed in Connecticut was Croton in 1705, through the labors of Valentine Wightman. The first in New Hampshire is claimed to be that at Dover in 1838 by Hanserd Knolleys. In Vermont a church was formed at Shaftsbury in 1768. The first church in South Carolina was constituted of William Scraven, a Baptist Minister and Deacon Humphry Churchwood and eight others, fleeing from persecution in Maine. They formed a church in Charleston of which Mr. Scraven became pastor. In Pennsylvania the Baptist were first organized at Cold Springs, near Bristol in Bucks caunty. Lower Dublin church, the mother of Philadelphia churches, was formed at Pennepek in 1688. Elias Keach was their first minister, who was the son of the famous Benjamin Keach of London.

The Philadelphia Association was formed in 1707, consisting at first, of but five churches, viz: Lower Dublin, Piscataway, Middletown, Cohansey and Welsh Tract.

Baptist churches have held and they do hold the independence of each individual church as the highest authority, an authority from whose decisions there can be no appeal. Under the New Testament model and Laws of Jesus Christ, each local church, be they many or few, only a dozen, or thousands of members associated or covenanted together in the faith of the gospel, and taking the New Testament as their law and Christ as their head have the right to a bishop or bishops, or pastors to watch over and feed them, and to make decisions in the settlement of church troubles and exerercises of christian privileges that no Council, Association, Synod, Assembly, Conference or Diocese can set set aside.

Parity in church government, instead of episcopacy, is what Baptists hold to and practice; so when the churches became numerous enough, after carefully guarding against the assumption of ecclesiastical power, and avoiding all interference with the affairs of individual churches, formed a Yearly Meeting, consisting of messengers and ministers from the different churches, and exercised a brotherly supervision over the Baptist cause and often devised, by such union of churches, liberal things on its behalf.

By such annual gatherings christian friendships was renewed and extended; important questions of doctrine and practice were discussed, and advice given in difficult cases; weak and destitute churches were assisted; and plans for the wider diffusion of gospel truth were originated.

Such a gathering as here explained finally grew into the Philadelphia Association at the time afore stated, the first in America.

From Welsh Tract church, a minister by the name of Paul Palmer constituted the first church in North Carolina, at Perquimans about the year 1727. But to the labors of Shuball Stearns and his companions, from the year 1854, must be attributed, under God, the extensive spread of Baptist views and practices, and the remarkable revival of religion by which the eighteenth century was distinguished.

Elder Stearns settled at Sandy Creek, North Carolina, in 1755, where a church by the name of Sandy Creek was soon organized consisting of sixteen members. This church soon increased to 606 members and may be justly styled the Mother of all the churches now included in the Southern Baptist Convention. Soon other churches were organized and in 1758 Sandy Creek Association was organized, being the third Baptist Association in America.

Daniel Marshall, the brother-in-law of Mr. Stearns was one of the most successful preachers of his time. He went on preaching tours in different states or colonies and other zealous men of God pierced the wilderness, the Lord attended the word spoken, and men and women were converted and churches built, until at the end of seventeen years after Sandy Creek church was formed, she had become the mother and grand-mother of forty-two churches, planting the Baptist banner eastward to the sea, westward to the Mississippi river, north to the Potomac and south to Georgia.

BAPTIST-CHURCHES AND ASSOCIATIONS IN WESTERN N. C.

Baptist operations commenced in Western North Carolina with the commencement of the Nineteenth century, so to speak.

Associated with the beginnings here are the names of the following Baptist ministers:

Thomas Snelson, Thomas Justice, Sion Blythe, Benjamin King, Humphry Posey and Stephen Morgan.

The first churches were Little Quay, Locust Field, New Found, Caney River. French Broad and Cane Creek.

The first three churches, named here formerly belonged to the Holston Association, Tennessee, and the latter three belonged to Broad River Association, South Carolina. In 1807, these six churches withdrew from the mother bodies and formed French Broad Association-

Touching the origin or age of the churches forming the French Broad Association, we have no account given except that of Locust Field which was organized in 1803. The Holston Association, from which came Little Ivey, Locust Field and New Found churches was really a daughter of the Sandy Creek Association.

A body of ministers and churches formed a semi-annual Conference in 1781 and acted under the supervision of Sandy Creek Association until 1786, when, on account of remoteness from the mother body, they formed the Holston Association. This body owed it's origin largely to Sandy Creek and a few ministers from Virginia. Rev. Tidance Lane was in the Baptist colony from N. C.

The three churches. Cove Creek. Caney River and French Broad, rom Broad River Association. South Carolina, doubtless received their rigin from the churches which had spread abroad from Sandy Creek, . C., and Charleston. South Carolina, and those old original communities or churches and Associations from England and Wales, either irectly or indirectly. Thus with the ministers and churches named he French Broad Association had its origin.

Tuckaseige Association was organized of churches from French Broad at Cullowhee church in 1829. The oldest churches were Locust Field, Cullowhee, Scotts Creek, Waynesville, Savannah, Cowee and Franklin. Coming farther west there is the Valley Association organized in 1839, first known as Nottey river etc. Valley River church, we think, was a member of the Valley Association, however a few hurches in Cherokee and some in Ga. formed said Association. So we term it that the Tennessee River Association is a great-granddaughter of French Broad on a part of the Tennessee river churches and a grand-daughter in part. No evil is done to the matter of our history if it be recorded that Tennessee River as it now stands is truly a daughter of Tuckasiege Association.

Chapter III.

MT. ZION CHURCH, 1829.

First Baptist efforts in the territory now included in Tennessee River Baptist Association began with the year 1829 which is noted as the time in which Mount Zion Baptist church was formed a few hundred yards from the Arneechee ford of Ocona Lufty, on the northwest side of the river. This church was built by Elders Humphry, Posey and Adam Corn, and beyond a doubt, the first Baptist effort in the present limits of The Tennessee River Baptist Association.

Local convenience for the people and brethren on Ocona Lufty, and for the people and brethren at Shoal Creek made it necessary for this church to divide after a few years, and in April or May 1836, the division was effected for the purpose of organizing Shoal Creek and Lufty, which soon followed. Thus the name of Mt. Zion disappears and her membership lives in Shoal Creek and Lufty. Some of the older Becks, Conners, Mingus, etc., were of the first membership in this old church. It was in this church that Elder Samuel Gibson was ordained to the work of the gospel ministry in 1834 by David Elder and Adam Corn. He was baptised into this church by Adam Corn in Ocona Lufty in 1830 and represented the church when it belonged to French Broad Association.

BRUSH CREEK CHURCH, 1832.

Brush creek was organized in December 1832, with eighteen members, viz. Joseph Sherrill and David Elder as Deacons, Thomas Hedgecock, Nathan DeHart, Nathan Tabor, George Loudermilk, Ute Sherrill, Susanah Truitt, Mary Edwards, Martha Hedgecock, Isabella Shoap, Nancy A. Hightower, Mary Truitt, Margaret Welch, Susanah Elder, Elisabeth Burns and Hanah, a colored woman.

Elder Humphrey Posey, Robert Byers and Peter Keykendall were the presbytery who constituted this church.

Brush Creek was admitted as a member of Tuckasiege Association where it remained until Sept. 1866 when it joined Friendship Association. This church has been the honored mother and grand-mother of others notably, Cold Spring, and others It has had the honor of being the pioneer body of Baptists on Tennessee River in all the southwest part of what is now Swain county. Here we find the worthy pioneer Baptists on Tennessee River in all the southwest part of what is now Swain county. Here we find the worthy pioneer Baptists Tabors, Levi Truitt, DeHarts, and Thomassons, Solomon Truitt, John DeHart and J. M. Thomasson were made deacons. David Elder, Allen Ammons and J. R. Edwards made ministers. Elders Humphrey Posey, Robert Byers and Peter Keykendall were the presbytery who constituted Brush Creek church. Posey was the first pastor of Brush Creek church, being chosen Jan. 1833.

LUFTY CHURCH, 1836.

Lufty Baptist church was constituted June 6, 1836, by Adam Corn and David Elder as presbytery, at the house of Dr. John Mingus on the west prong of the river, Lufty, with the following members:

Robert Collins and Ephraim Mingus, Deacons, Jacob Mingus Abreham Mingus, Jacob Mingus, Sr. John Beck, Jacob Beck, Samuel Beck, Samuel Conner and John Watson, and females, Sophia Mingus, Sarah Mingus, Rebecca Mingus, Elizabeth Collins, Jane Beck, Nancy Beck, Cyntha Beck, Susanah Watson, Nancy Conner, Massy Conner and Elizabeth Stillwell.

This church made application and was received into Tuckaseige Baptist Association in the session held with Cowee church in August 1836, Robert Collins and Jaccb Mingus being the first delegation to the Association.

Lufty church has been the birth place of some of the most noted preachers and members of Western North Carolina. Elder C. B. Mingus was born and reared, converted to the Lord, and commenced preaching here. A very interesting career has been given to Lufty church and many precious names have been added to this church among the departed and survivors whose names are doubtless in the book of life. The greatest conflict she ever had to endure was the rent in her membership, caused by the so-called preaching of one Sam Castile about the year 1873. Our soul heaves a melanchollv sigh when we think of this schism in this dear old church. More then twenty-five of her members were lead off into Castleism and had to be excluded. This trouble gave rise to bitter feelings among neighbers that has never, nor will ever be healed on time's side of eternity. Leaders in this struggle for the Master's cause against the corruption of he Castile doctrine were the zealous Elders W. H. Conner, and Deacon H. J. Beck by whose efforts, by the blessing of God, the church : rid of Castile and his followers.

CHEOAH BAPTIST CHURCH, 1848.

Cheoah church was organized July 18th 1848, by Elders Baily Bruce and James Kimsey, travelling missionaries under the auspices of the Baptist State Convention of North Carolina. This church was organized with eighteen members of whom John Hyde and Thomas Ammons were made Deacons.

As Cheoah was the first Baptist church in the valley of the same name, it became the nucleus of Baptist operations for more than half of what is now Graham county, N. C , and is either the mother or grand-mother of several of the neighboring churches.

The labors of Bruce and Kimsey in this valley are hallowed by many precious names; John Hyde, Thomas Ammons, Jacob Davis, william Davis, William Carpenter and others who have been distinguished Baptist christians of great moral worth. The Cheoah church was a member of Tuckasiege Association until August 1871, when it was dismissed to become a member of a new Association, organized in October 1861. We presume that Yellow Creek, Sweet Water, and Love Oak churches are daughters of Cheoah church.

TENNESSEE RIVER CHURCH.

Tennessee River Baptist church was organized with ten members, in the year 1835, by Elders James Kinzey and David Elkey, the name of Stecoah, and contained in it members residing in the Stecoah Valley as well as members along Chamber's Creek and Tennessee River. This church was also a member of Tuckasiege Association.

The church roll of the first members cannot be given, but we call to memory some precious names among the pioneer Baptists of the settlement in which the Tennessee River is located, and men who have been prominent in her past membership; viz: Joseph Welch, Pendleton Crisp, John Chambers, John Hyde and others. The Welchs, Crisp and Chambers have long since slept with their fathers, but old brother John Hyde, holding the office of Deacon, and whose name is found on the roll of Lufty church, as well as that of Cheoah is still (Jan. 29, 1891) living at over 95 years of age in the Cheoah valley, but Bro. Hyde has been blind for many years. He was a man strong in the faith and a soul-bracer to young christians. We well remember some sweet impressions made upon the writers mind by this dear old father in Isreal.

STECOAH CHURCH, 1850.

A loss of the first part of the church record prevents our giving the names of the members and presbytery who organized the Stecoah Baptist church but according to account given by brother W. D. Crisp, one of her most prominent members, this church was formed in the year 1850, under the name of New Prospect, which name it retained until it was changed to its present name. It joined the Tuckasiege Association, where it remained until dismissed to go into the organization of the Friendship Baptist Association. This church has had an honorable career in our Baptist ranks. It was the homeof the venerable John L. Crisp, where he labored as a member and a worthy minister of the gospel until death. Simson Crisp and others of the Crisp name have lived and died here.

Deacon J. C. Owensby was an honored Deacon of Stecoah church, who died in his 47th year. Old brother A. Taylor, one of the most intelligent and best informed Baptists had his membership in Stecoah church for several years, and was a very prominent man in the affairs of the churches of his country.

COLD SPRING BAPTIST CHURCH.

Cold Spring Baptist church was constituted May 2nd 1851, by Elders I. T. S. Sherrill, Samuel Gibson and Allen Ammons, with the following members, viz; John DeHart and M. Hedgecock, Deacons, Nathan DeHart. Hilary Scott, A. W. Davis, Elizabeth Hedgecock, Katherine DeHart and Mira Davis.

This church was built chiefly of members from Brush Creek church

Although so small a beginning, this church was increased at its next or second meeting by the following named members:

B. H. Elder and wife, Nancy A., Martha Hedgecock, John D. Brenle and wife, Charlott, Jessee Smiley and wife, Elizabeth, John Jenkins, Martin DeHart. Sarah Scott and Katherine Scott, all by letters, making the total membership nineteen for the organic period.

The church joined the Tuckaseige Association in Aug. 1851, John DeHart, M. Hedgecock and B. H. Elder being the delegates to that body.

The first pastors were Samuel Gibson, I. T. S. Sherrill, Allen Ammons and Jacob Mingus all called to serve the first year, three months each in rotation—Elder Jacob Mingus to serve the first quarter.

Cold Spring church, for several years, numbered in her membership, Elder I. T. S. Sherrill, who served her several years as pastor, or bishop. his service as early as 1855, Elders Gibson and Ammons, heretofore named, have served as bishops, divers years. The eloquent Merit Rickman served this church a few terms prior to 1860, by whose service the young church was ably led. Elder A. A. Justice whose pastoral service commenced with the church during the late Rebelion of the States served longer than any other man.

By the untiring labors of Elder Justice, the church has had some of the most precious meetings and ingatherings to its membership. A noted revival was held by Justice in August, 1865, which greatly built up the church. The greatest revival of religion, ever known in the church and community were the series that took place during the months of

July and August 1876, during which more than forty were added to the church of Baptism and about thirty by letter.

The preaching on the August occasion was done by Elders Richard Evans and James Salts of Sevier county, Tennessee, whose labors were continued two sermons a day for about ten days. Elder Justice was pastor at this time and aided, as did Elder J. M. Smiley.

Of the churches, Valley River, Valleytown, and Murphy of Cherokee county, and Nantahala of Macon county, being four of the six churches which participated in the organization of the Friendship Association at Valleytown, in October 1861, we know but little of their history antedating the Association; and, consequently, as they have all four withdrawn from the body and belong to other Associations—we will not, (owing to lack of information,) tax these pages by endeavoring to follow them from their organizations, as we have the other churches which existed in the present bounds of Tennessee River Association, being the counties of Swain and Graham and Tellico church in Macon county, and prior to the formation of the Association, in 1861, but will, with this passing notice, say that the above named churches formed an important basis upon which the present Association, known as Tennessee River, has been built.

In the pages following the account of the organization of the Association will be found noted incidents of the churches and noble brethren who have left us and joined other Associations.

CHAPTER IV, 1861.

ORGANIZATION OF FRIENDSHIP BAPTIST ASSOCIATION.

Having gone through a brief narrative of the churches and Baptist history, in the territory of the Association, previous to its existence we now cronicle the organization and endeavor to follow the chain of events as they have transpired since the churches formed into an Association.

The Convention, for such was the first meeting called, consisting of delegates from six churches, viz: Valley River—Elders Mark May Wiley Philips, and brethren James Whitaker. Sen. and James Whitaker. Jr.

Valley Town—Elder James Kimsey and brethren L. Gosnel and W. A. Parker.

Nantahala—M. '. Lunsford.

Cheoah—W. B. Wiggins.

Murphy—J. L. Johnson.

Fort Lindsey—A. A. Justice, eleven delegates in all, met with Valley Town church on Valley River, in Cherokee county, N. C., Oct. 25 and 26, 1861, and organized the Friendship Baptist Association.

Adopting Articles of Faith and Rules of Decorum for the guidance of the Association, were among the most important transactions of this first session. The infant body opened correspondence with other Associations adjoining its territory.

No statistical table was published: therefore, the number of members in the churches cannot be given. As the little body was coeval with the war of Secession, but little could be expected till that struggle was over.

According to the official announcement of Moderator, James Kimsey, and the Clerk, Mark May, the meeting of this convedtion actually organized the Friendship Baptist Association with but four churches; Valley River, Valley Town, Murphy and Cheoah; but as before stated A. A. Justice, from Fort Lindsey, and brother Lindsford from Nantahala, participated in the Convention, as it was called,

We are satisfied, however, that Nantahala church, near the flats of Nantahala, was truly a constituent member of the organization, but as to Fort Lindsey, we think it died, and was never again represented in the Association.

If a vestage of that church lives at the present time, it is in the person of old brother Aaron Miller and probably two or three other members in subsequent organizations or churches called Nantahala and Wesser Creek, which names appear farther on in this work.

To show how Baptists, and especially those fathers of our Associaation, held in regard to the faith of the Baptists, and how they hold in regard to the powers and duties of Associations, we here insert, in full and verbatim, The Articles of Faith and Rules of Decorum which is the Constitution of the Association which they adopted at the first meeting at Valley Town.

ARTICLES OF FAITH.

1. "We believe in one only living and true God, and that there are three persons in the Godhead: the Father, the Son, and the Holy Ghost, and that these three are one.

2. We believe the Scriptures of the Old and New Testaments are the word of God and the only true rule of word and practice.

3. We believe in the doctrine of original sin.

4. We believe in man's incompetency to recover himself from the fallen state he is in by nature, and that justification in the sight of God is only obtained by the righteousness of Jesus Christ.

5. We believe in the doctrine of election through sanctification of the Spirit and belief of the truth.

6. We believe that saints shall persevere in grace, and that none of them shall ever fall away and be lost.

7. We believe in the resurrection of the dead and a general judgment, and that the punishment of the wicked and joys of the righteous shall be eternal.

8. We believe that Baptism and the Lord's Supper are ordinances instituted by Christ, and that true believers are the only proper subjects thereof.

9. We believe the only true mode of Baptism is Immersion.

10. We believe that none have a right to administer the ordinances but Ministers of the Gospel regularly ordained to that office.

RULES OF DECORUM.

1 The Association shall be composed of male members chosen by the churches which they represent, who shall produce certificates of their appointment, accompanied with a statement of the number in their respective churches, of those Baptised, received by letter, dismissed, excluded, restored and dead, during the previous year, with the whole number in fellowship.

2 The members thus convened shall have no power to Lord it over God's Heritage, nor shall they infringe on any of the internal rights of any church in the Union.

3 The Association shall have a Moderator and Clerk, (which last shall also be Treasurer), who shall be chosen by the suffrages of the members present, and shall continue in office until a new appointment is made.

4 The Moderator shall preserve order, and call to its observance at any time. He shall have the privilege of leaving his seat, provided the chair be filled, and of engaging in debate.

5 The Clerk shall minute the proceedings of the Association; prepare them for the press: keep a file of the printed minutes present at each session, for the use of the body, and deliver them over to his successor. He shall also take charge of the money and other property belonging to the Association and dispose of them as the body shall direct.

6 In the decision of any question, a majority of votes shall deter-

mine the point.

7. The Association shall always be opened and closed by prayer.

8. Each member of the Association will be expected to be in his place at the hour of meeting, on each day of the session, and remain until the dismission of the body,

9. Any member wishing to speak shall rise from his seat and address the Moderator; he shall attend close to his subject; shall make no remarks on the slips or blunders of any who spoke before him. If two or more rise at the same time, the Moderator shall name the one to speak first.

10. No member shall absent himself in time of business, without leave from the Moderator.

11. No member shall speak more than three times on the same subject without leave.

12. We admit of no other title than Brother when engaged in business.

13. Every motion made and seconded shall come under the consideration of the Association, except it be withdrawn by the mover.

14. Corresponding messengers will be considered as members of this body, and entitled to the privileges of the same.

15. Ministering brethren present not belonging to this Associaiion, may be invited to seats, but not to vote.

16. Every query sent by any church in our Union shall be attended to, if it appears in the church letter, and the Association shall answer it if considered agreeable to good order.

17. The Association has power to withdraw from any church which deviates from the orthodox principles of the Gospel or fellowships disorder.

18. The minutes shall be read, and correetected if need be, and signed by the Moderator and Clerk before the Association rises.

19. Any church wishing to be admitted into this Association may petition by letter and delegates, and if orthodox and orderly, shall be received, and their reception made manifest by the Moderator giving them the right hand and inviting them to seats.

20. The Association may appoint any member or members, by and with their consent, as committees, or otherwise, to transact any business which they may think proper.

21. This Association will appreciate and encourage a sound ministry while she will cry down an unsound and disorderly one.

22. This Association shall not send help to any church in our Union by authority of an Association, but advise churches to apply to sister churches for help if necessary.

23. The Association may adjourn at any time which they may think proper. Amendments to this plan or form of government may be made at any time by a majority of the Association, upon the conclusion of the whole: We assume no higher power or authority than the Advisory council."

The first session of the Association was held with Valley Town church and transacted its business, we suppose, according to the appointment made by the organizing convention, which was to take place on Friday before the second Sunday in October, 1862.

We think Elder James Kimsey was Moderator, and from a report of a special committee made to the Association at its session in 1864, we know that brother A. Taylor was Clerk.

As the minutes of this session were never printed, we have but a meagre knowledge of the history for the year 1862.

We see by subsequent account of this matter that the failure to have the minutes printed for 1862, was attributable to brother Taylor, the Clerk.

It is proper to say that two churches were admitted into the Association at the session of 1862, viz: New Hope, in Clay county, N. C., and New Prospect, subsequently named Stecoah, in Cherokee county, N. C.

As to the progress of the churches for this year, we cannot speak, as there are no statistics given in the minutes.

In 1863 the Association was to have met with New Prospect church, and according to account given in the minutes for 1864, Valley River, Valley Town, New Hope and Cheoah, through their delegates, got together, but in consequence of hostile parties of men raiding and plundering the country about New Prospect, it was decided not to enter into the business of an Association.

It was at this session, the failure of which we have shown, that Cold Spring Baptist church was to join the young Association, as appears from the records of said church. A. W. Davis and J. M. Smiley were elected delegates to hear the petition for admission, but the minutes of the Association do not show that Cold Spring ever joined.

Again, the name of Stecoah appears in the minutes, or first statistical table ever printed, being that of 1865, but when and where it joined the Friendship Association is not shown in the minutes, but we think it likely that this church which was afterward named Tennessee River, as will be seen further on, joined or was to have joined the Association, in 1863, at New Brospect church, but the failure to hold the Association that year, has cause of loss of the account of those two churches joining the body.

The Association met in 1864 with Valley River church on Saturday, Oct. 8th, and was in session three days. Elder James Kimsey preached the Introductory from Thess. 5th chapt.

A delegation from a few of the churches assembled and organized the body by appointing James Whitaker Sr., Moderator, and Charles N. George, Clerk.

This session did but litttle business. Appointing its accustomed correspondence to sister Associations, adopting a most excellent circular letter written by James Whitaker, Sr., on the subject of the Christian warfare, setting forth a preamble or report showing the failure of the session of 1863 and failure to get the minutes printed for 1862, and instructing brother George to hunt up said manuscript and money which he failed to find, was about all the business done this session save appointing the time, place, and preacher for the Association in 1865, which was to convene at New Hope church in Clay county, North Carolina.

As there is no statistical table for this year we can say but little for the progress of the body, but we infer that the number of churches participating in the Association for 1864 and those which had become connected with the young body up to this time, as the minutes for 1865 lead us to believe, there were Valley River, Valley Town, Cheoah, New Hope, Murphy, Nantahala, New Prospect, Cold Spring and Stecoah, with a total membership not exceeding two hundred and fifty.

The great Secession war had prostrated, and demoralized the whole country, so that churches suffered from its distressing consequences and Zion languished throughout our bounds. The Whitakers, Elder Kimsey, and a few other old brethren and sisters who were not called to the front in the struggle, remained at their post at home and watched and prayed for Zion and the welfare of the country, but revivals were few and small.

CHAPTER V.

The fourth, or rather the fifth session, counting the meeting which organized the body, was held with New Hope church, Clay county, N. C., September 8th and 9th, 1865. The Introductory was preached by Elder James Kimsey. James Whitaker Sr., was the Moderator and J. A. Kimsey Clerk.

The great Secession war was ended, but the prostrate condition of the country, caused by the evils following such troubles was felt in every institution, churches as well as all others. Mail facilities were such that but little could be learned or communicated save what passed orally from person to person and the whole southern country was one sad spectacle of poverty and ruin; consequently, there was but little money to start with, to begin anew to revive, upon the ruins of this much devasted country, the noble schools and churches which had suffered so much by the shock of war.

The Friendship Associatio held this fifth session with only five of her nine churches represented, viz: Valley River, James Whitaker Sr. and James Whitaker Jr., Elder W. Philips.

Cheoah—C. N George and William Deaver.

Valley Town—Brother Taylor, Elder Kimsey and J. A. Kimsey.

New Hope—Isaac Watts, and two more brethren, Garrison and Watts.

Murphy—James Johnson,* twelve delegates.

There was neither delegates or reports from Nantahala, New Prospect, Cold Spring and Stecoan churches.

Elder E. Hedden, Hiawassee Association, Eld. J. B. Parham and brethren Isaac Flemming and A. H. Hampton from Nantahala River were present as corresponding messengers.

As to the usual business transactions of the body, they consisted of organization after reading letters from the churches, receiving correspondence to other Associations and send corresponding letters.

Appoint Introductory preacher and time and place for succeeding session, hear and consider reports of committes, etc.

The Association for 1865, made its first attempt to organize Sunday schools by appointing a committee on the subject and passing a resolution instructing the churches to organize Sunday schools where they could get suitable teachers.

The contribution for minutes, being $8.52, was the only financial report.

There had been three baptisms in Valley River during the Associational year, one by letter was received in each of the churches, Cheoah and Valley Town, three restored into the fellowship of Valley River.

One death in Cheoah and one death in Murphy with a standing total membership in the five churches represented of 128. Taking those four churches not represented in 1865 and the whole membership cannot be safely estimated at exceeding three hundred.

Thus with three ministers, viz: James Kimsey, Mark May and Wiley Philips and this small membership scattered over part of Cherokee, Clay and Macon counties, N. C., did the Friendship Baptist Association emerge from the distracting war times.

In the year 1866 a brighter day of prosperity and growth dawned upon the Association.

The annual session was held with Valley River church 7th and 8th of September 1866

James Whitaker Sr., was Moderator, and J. A. Kimsey, Clerk. Elder J. B. Parham, of Notolah Association had been appointed to preach the Introductory sermon, which place he filled with one of the best of efforts. At this session every church was represented by delegates, except Murphy, and it sent a letter and statistics. Thirty-four delegates were present. Brush Creek church from Tuckasiege Association was recieved by letter, adding Allen Ammons and A. A. Justice to the list of ordained ministers and seventy-five members.

Panther Creek church organized in —— 1866 by Elders ———— was recieved with its delegates, Louis Medlin and son, L. M. Medlin, adding a membership of thirteen.

Peaceful Traveller, an Indian church newly organized with a membership of sixteen, was also recieved and Elder John Shell, their preacher, was added to the list of ministers. This later church was also dismissed in a body to go to the Indian Territory which they subsequently did.

There had been fifty-three persons baptized during the year, two in Valley River church, one in Murphy, thirty-one in Cold Spring, six in Stecoah and one in Peaceful Traveller.

Twenty had been recieved by letter in all the churches; seventeen excluded, six restored, thirty-three dismissed and one died, total membership four hundred and five.

The usual committees for this sixth session were Arrangements, Preaching, Finance and Sunday schools.

Correspondence were recieved from Hiawassee Association by Elder E. Hedden, from Notly Association by Elder J. B. Parham and from Tuckasige Association Elders Samuel Gibson and A. A. Justice, and correspondence was appointed in return to those bodies.

An attempt was made to have the life and writings of James Whitaker, Sr., published in book form by appointing a joint committee on this business to act in concert with a committee from Hiawassee Association.

Friendship committee—Elders James Kimsey and C. N. George and James Whitaker, Jr.

A favorable report of the committee was made at a future session and a biographer or writer engaged but so far as we are informed the work was never published.

As it was customary for the Associations to have Circular letters written to be printed in their minutes, it fell to the lot of old brother James Whitaker, Sr., this year on the subject of "Brotherly Love."

Noble effort, indeed, did he make and closed his letter with the following rhyme which was his own production:

"'Tis love that rules the Christian's heart,
Both near at home, and far apart,
The body thus of Christ they are
And members in particular.

Then if a brother should transgress,
A secret dealing God will bless,
Go to Him and his faults make known,
Between Himself and thee alone.

And if he hear thee, well and good.
His sin is washed in Jesus' blood,
Your brother thus restored to you,
Your love to Him should still be true.

But if he should neglect to hear,
Distressing thought for you to bear,
To see your labor prove in vain,
Your brother in his sins remain.

But mind the rule our Lord has sent,
The second time he may repent,
And if he does forgive him then,
As God forgives the sons of men.

Take with you, one or two beside,
And pray the Lord to be your guide,
And tell him in a loving strain.
The place you think his sins remain.

Perhaps the two you take along,
May be the means to show his wrong,
Then joyful if the Lord should bless,
Your brother with discerning grace.

But if he still unfeeling prove,
Let faithfulness be joined with love,
For in the Gospel field we know,
One other step does plainly show,

The Church, that body, sacred place,
Must hear your much distressing case.
Likewise a full decision give,
That every child of God may live.

But if the church he will not hear,
He's in his sins, but you are clear;
Then unto thee, let him remain,
And heathen and a publican."

"The session for 1866, ended in love and prosperity. Elder Kimsey was made to express his joy at the thought of the added strength in ministers and members.

The following is the list of churches with delegations as sent to this session which was held with Valley River church:

Valley River—W. Philips, James Whitaker, Sr., and James Whitaker, Jr.

Cheoah—Wm. Deaver, Jacob Davis, W. Sumpter, and C. N George.

Valley Town—James Kimsey and J. A. Kimsey.

Nantahala—M. May, G. W. Yonce, M. Lunsford and J. Fouts.

New Hope—Isaac Watts.

New Prospect—John Hyde, J. C. Owensby, J, L. Crisp and M. B, Crisp.

Murphy—By letter.

Cold Spring—John DeHart, J. S. Smiley and M. Cockerham.

Stecoah—P. Crisp, B. L. Sawyer, Robert Crisp.

Brush Creek—A. Ammons, A. A. Justice, H. Manly, D. Wall and B. McHan.

Panther Creek—L. Medlin and L. M. Medlin.

Peaceful Traveler—John Snell, G. F. Morris and D. M. Morris.

The Association year, 1867, was not characterized by any very notable events, and there was a fall off in the total membership from 405 to 377.

Peaceful Traveler church had gone to Indian Territory, and no church had joined the Association.

This year the Association met with Cold Spring church, then in Macon county, N. C., and was in session three days, commencing Friday, Sept. 6th.

The venerable James Kimsey preached the Introductory from 2 Tim. 4: and latter clause of 7 verse.

Elder Kimsey was Moderator and his son, Joseph A. Kimsey, Cle Only nineteen messengers were present at this session. From Vall River church, James Whitaker, Jr., and B. F. Adams; from Cheoa C. N. George, William Deaver, William Sumpter, and G. W. Hoope from Valley Town, James Kimsey and J. A. Kimsey; from Nant hala, M. Barnes; from New Prospect, J. C. Owenby; from Cold Sprin John DeHart, John Earls and M. Cockerham; from Stecoah, Pendl ton Crisp; from Brush Creek, A. Ammons, J. M. Thomasson, J. Edwards and S. J. Freeman; from Panther Creek, Louis Medlin an J. L. Proctor, and from Murphy and New Hope no delegates. Ne Hope church was never again represented and was lost to the Ass ciation, but from what cause we are not informed.

Twenty-six had been added to the churches by baptism, viz: T Valley River, two; Cheoah, four; Nantahala, fourteen; Cold Sprin one; Brush Creek, four; Panther Creek, one. In all the churches, 3 were received by letter, 32 dismissed, 13 excluded, 2 restored, and fo died during the year.

Only three committees were appointed at this session. On Arrang ments—Elder A. Ammons, James Whitaker, Jr., C. N. George ar Moderator and Clerk.

Preaching—John Dehart, Wm. Deaver and L. Medlin.

Finance—William Sumpter and J. M. Thomasson.

Nothing was raised for any object, except twenty dollars for prin ing the minutes of the Association. Corresponding Messengers wl visited inthe little Association 1867, Elders Samuel Gibson, Meri Rickman, and brethren P. G. Green, W P. Allison, from Tuckasei Association, and Elder E. A. Deweese, from Liberty Association..

Correspondence was appointed to the several Associations, Tuck seige, Hiwassee, Liberty and Notley. Union Meetings were appointe one in each of three Union Districts into which the Association ha been divided. These meetings were for the discussion of Ministeri and Deacons' duties and other points of doctrine and church disci line

Two Queries were sent up to the Association, which were answer in the negative. A query from New Prospect church in these words:

"Is it Bible order for a church to call a supply out ot her bounds, when she has an ordained minister in her own church?"

Query from Valley River: "Is it good order for churches in our Union to receive members under their watch-care and then grant said members letters of dismission?"

The body received a favorable report from the Book Committee on the Life and Writings of James Whitaker, Sen., and appointed two Agents to raise funds for the publication of the work.

Thus the workings of the churches and Association, for 1867, passed into history, as nothing more of importance took place except the adoption of a Circular Letter by James Whitaker, Sen., taking ground that Moses was translated instead of dying.

The year 1868, had been more prosperous than the year previous. The Association met in its seventh anniversary with New Prospect church. Elder Kimsey was Moderator and James Whitaker, Jr., Clerk.

Elder A. Ammons preached the Introductory from Eph. 4:4.

MESSENGERS OR DELEGATES.

Valley River—James Whitaker, Jr., Hyatt, E. E. Sharp.

Cheoah—Jacob Davis, Joshua Gibson, William Carpenter, G. W. Hooper, William Davis.

Valley Town—Rev. James Kimsey.

Nantahala—Rev. Mark May, M. Barnes, Joseph Stepp.

New Prospect—J. L. Crisp, J. C. Owensby, W. A. Crisp.

Cold Spring—J. M. Smiley.

Stecoah—P. Crisp.

Brush Creek— Elder Allen Ammons, H. Manley, D. Wall, W R. Simonds, J. M. Thomasson.

Panther Creek—W. Proctor, L. Medlin, J. C. Proctor,

Alarka—R. M, Roberts, J. T. Upton.

Buffalo—Colonawheska, Elam, (Indians.)

Murphy church was not represented.

Alarka church had been organized in Feb. 1868, by Elders Samuel

Gibson and Meritt Rickman with nine members, and was recieved into the Association at the session of 1868, which commenced October 3rd, and Buffalo, and Indian church was recieved by letter from Hiawassee Association. Nantahala church was dismissed from the Association by which it sustained a loss of forty-four members and one of its ablest ministers, viz: M. May.

But three standing committees were appointed at this session.

Arrangements—Elder A. Ammons, J. M. Smiley, J. L. Crisp.

Preaching—J. Davis, D. Wall, Ute Hyatt, J. L. Crisp, J. C. Owensby.

Finance—J. M- Thomasson and William Carpenter.

Merritt Rickman, Samuel Gibson, W. Deweese, P. R. Rickman and J. D. Franks were received as messengers from Tuckaseige Association, and Berry Chastain as a messenger from Hiwassee Association, S. M. McCurley from Notley and M. S. Hall from Liberty. Fraternal relations were reciprocated by appointing messengers to all the above named Baptist Associations. Appointing Union Meetings, adopting a Circular letter by James Whitaker, Sr., on the subject of "Brotherly Love," recommending churches to hold prayer meeting, adopting a resolution to patronize Tuckaseige Baptist High School at Holly Spring in Macon Co., N. C., and a report of the Book Committee, report on Finance and some other matters were about all that engaged the attention of the session.

The Book Committee's report was still favorable as to the Life and Writings of old brother Whitaker, but the funds, owing to hard times, had not been raised to print it, but a compiler of the book, M R. Kimsey, Esq., had been engaged, and with this the matter of publishing Father Whitaker's Life and Writings ended, so far as the Association was concerned.

Twenty members had been added to Valley River church by baptism, and twenty-nine by baptism in all the churches of the Association. Twenty-five received by letter, twenty-seven dismissed, nineteen excluded, four restored, and four died, during the year, leaving a total membership of 465.

Nothing on the subject of Sunday schools or Missions had been attempted, and no ministers had been ordained, and with the loss of Elder May, the ordained ministers were James Kimsey, Allen Ammons and Wiley Philips, according to our best information.

The Association met with Valley River church in its Eighth Session and was in session four days, commencing Oct. 1st.

Elder Kimsey preached the Introductory from Ezra 8:9.

James Whitaker, Sr., James Whitaker, Jr., James McBrayer and Ute Hyatt, from Valley River; J. Davis, Wm. Gunter, C. Hudson, L. Farr and brother Brooks, from Cheoah; James Kimsey, Valley Town; J. R. Lindsay, Murphy; J. M. Smiley, Cold Spring; John Hyde, Tennessee River; R. M. Roberts, Alarka; A. Ammons, Brush Creek; William Proctor, Panther Creek; Cullowheskee, Tetoheske, Buffalo, constituted the delegation. New Prospect was not represented.

James Kimsey was Moderator and James Whitaker, Jr., Clerk. An able minister by the name of James Underwood from Ellijay Association, Ga., was present as a Transient minister, and rendered valuable aid to the body. Correspondence from Tuckaseige Association, Elder Joshua Ammons and his son John Ammons, and Elders Alfred and Jesse Corn from Hiwassee.

This session widened the scope of its work by appointing more committees than usual, viz: a committee on Deceased Members and a committee on Sunday Schools.

Elder James McBrayer, of Valley River church, had moved into the bounds, and R. M. Roberts, of Alarka church, had been ordained in the month of June, increasing the list of ministers. The Association reduced the number of Union Meeting Districts to two.

The name of Stecoah church had been changed during the year to Tennessee River.

The custom of writing Corresponding Letters to sister Associations was kept up.

James Whitaker, Sr., had been the writer of the Circular Letter. This year it was on the subject the "Office and work of the Holy Spirit," but it was short, the writer confessing it to be too deep for his pen. The churches were advised at this session to endeavor to create a Church Fund to pay their preacher and other incidental expenses of the churches.

An earnest report on Sunday Schools was made by the committee, Elders Underwocod and A. Corn, urging the churches to look well to this branch of Christian duty, and recommend the people to purchase Sunday School books from the American Baptist Publication Society. Nothing had been done, prior to this, in the Association, or if so no reports of Sunday Schools were made by the churches to the body. The name of the Association was changed to Tennessee River.

Death had removed five of the members from the church militant. Sister Elizabeth Howell, 94 years of age and a member 78 years, had gone from Valley River. Also Charles N. George, 78 years of age, had passed away. Sister Sarah J. Kimsey, wife of Elder Kimsey and one of the model women, had gone.

Cheoah church had been blessed with a most glorious revival, and forty-three members were added to it by baptism. This work, under God, was the result of a protracted meeting held with this church of 18 days during October, 1868, by Elder A. Ammons, assisted by J. M. Smiley, a licentiate. Elder Ammons baptized thirty-three of these converts in twenty-five minutes.

Fifty-three had been baptized in all the churches, 52 received by letter, 43 dismissed, 19 excluded, 4 restored and 5 died, leaving the total membership of the Association 420.

Eighteen dollars for printing minutes made up the finance.

CHAPTER VI.

The Association is now known as Valley River.

With the year, 1870, a new era seems to have dawned upon the Association. The body met this year, Sept. 2nd with Cheoah church. Elder A. Ammons preached the Introductory from 1st Cor. 16:13. The death of Moderator Kimsey, made the Chair vacant at the opening of this sesion and A. Ammons was called to the Moderatorship for the first time. James Whitaker, Jr, was again chosen Clerk.

Ten churches were represented in this Council. New Hope still appears on the roll of churches, but without representation.

MESSENGERS FROM THE CHURCHES.

Elders Wiley Philips and James McBrayer, and James Whitaker, Jr. and Ute Hyatt, from Valley River: G. W. Hooper, Clinton Hudson, Jacob Davis, William Carpenter, Cheoah; M. Saunders from Murphy; J. M. Smiley, J. S. Smiley, Cold Spring; John Hyde, David Welch, Tennessee River; Elder R. M. Roberts, Alarka; A. Ammons, D. Wall, J. R. Edwards, Brush Creek; B. L. Morgan, M. Bradshaw, Panther Creek; J. L. Crisp, J. C. Owensby, R. H. Owensby, W. A. Crisp, Stecoah, which church had been changed in name from New Prospect to the present one in order to more definitely locate its situation. Buffalo was represented by Arquetake, Jesse Dickageeska. Valley Town church was not represented.

MESSENGERS FROM ASSOCIATIONS.

Elder Jesse Corn, J. R. Harrison, J. Taylor, W. M. Robinson, Hiawassee Association; J. B. Gibson, Tuckaseige Association.

BUSINESS COMMITTEES.

Arrangements—Jessee Corn, Ute Hyatt, D. Wall.

Preaching—J. L. Crisp, J. Davis, Ute Hyatt.

Changes, a term used instead of Deceased Members, upon which C. Hudson, J. C. Owensby and M. Launders were put as committee.

J. Corn, W. Philips, R. M. Roberts—Sunday schools.

Nine members had died during the year. The venerable James Kimsey, one of the giant men of the Association had closed his earthly career and Manos Morgan, 77 years old, of Panther Creek, and seven Indians of Buffalo church. Sabbath schools had taken a hopeful rise as there had been several among the churches during the year. As usual, correspondence with other Associations was kept up.

The Circular Letter, subject "Relative Duties of Churches and Ministers Pastors of Churches," was an able paper by James Whitaker, Sr. Also a sketch of the Life of James Kimsey was written by Father Whitaker to appear elsewhere.

Transient Ministers, I. T. Sherrill and Alfred Corn were present and did the Sunday preaching, Elder Sherrill making an unusually good effort carrying off the congregation.

The year 1870, was not noted for a large number of baptisms, there being only 28 in all the churches, the Indian church having baptized 10; Valley River comes next with 8 baptisms.

Total membership in all the churches, 483, a net gain of 63 during the year.

The year 1870 closed out with the following ministers:

A. Ammons, of Brush Creek, R. M. Roberts, of Alarka, Wiley Philips and James McBrayer, of Valley River, Elier Ratler, (Indian,) the ordained ministers.

Licentiates were J. M. Smiley, of Cold Spring, G. W. Hooper, of Cheoah and John James.

The tenth Anniversary, embracing the history of the Association 1 891 met with Brush Creek church, Swain county, N. C., Sept. 1st. Introductory sermon by R. M. Roberts from 2nd Cor. 6 :1.

The name of the Association having been changed from Friendship to Valley River, in 1869, now entered upon its second session under the new name. Allen Ammons was Moderator and James Whitaker, Jr. Clerk. Every church was represented, except Valley Town and it sent in a letter and statistics.

Messengers of the churches present were R. M. Roberts, John Wiggins, T. L. Passmore, Joseph Mason, P. H. Mason, Alarka church; A. Ammons, B. McHan, D. Wall, J. W. DeHart, Brush Creek church; Tahqutchee, H. Rathbone, Isaac Cheoah, Tahchanochutee, Indians from Buffalo; G. W. Hooper, J. Sherrill, J. Davis, Thomas Ammons, Cheoah; J. M. Smiley, J. M. Thomasson, John Earls, John DeHart, J. S. Panther, L. L. Thomasson, Cold Spring; Jesse Corn, J. R. Lindsay, William Sumpter, Murphy; W. Proctor, L. M. Medlin, B. L. Morgan, Panther Creek; J. L. Crisp, W. D. Crisp, M. A. Crisp, D. A. Taylor, Stecoah church; John Hyde, David Welch, W. F. Whiteside, P. Crisp, Tennessee River church; J. M. McBrayer,

V. Philips, Ute Hyatt, H. P. Adams, James Whitaker, Jr., Valley River. Messengers from sister Associations were M. May, Samuel Gibson, P. G. Green, J. D. Franks, H. J. Beck, J. M. Forester from Tuckaseige. David Owl from Liberty, and corresponding letters were received from Hiwassee and Notley Associations. The several committees were Jesse Corn, Ute Hyatt and J. D. Franks.—Arrangements.

Jacob Davis, B. McHan, W. Sumpter—Preaching.

R. M. Roberts, J. L. Crisp, L. M. Medlin —Sunday schools.

W. Philips, J. M. Thomasson, G. W. Hooper. Changes, J. M Smiley, William Proctor.—To write Corresponding Letters.

J. R. Lindsay, J. M. Thomasson, Pendleton Crisp—Finance.

Correspondence was kept up with other Associations.

Transient ministers present were I. T. S. Sherrill, holding a Letter of Dismission and A. A. Justice from Tuckasiege Association. Circular Letter by James Whitaker on "Ordinances of the Church" adopted and he continued to write a letter next year. Struck out the subject of Union meetings by which this very useful custom among the churches, which had previously been kept up in the Association, was discontinued for a time. Murphy church was dismissed to join Ducktown Association.

The *Cottage Visitor*, a Baptist paper published by Elder N. Bowen was reccommended by resolution, and the churches, by resolution, were advised to hold three Communion Services per annum. The year 1871, had been quite prosperous. Jesse Corn had moved into the bounds adding one more to the list of ordained ministers. Eighty-one persons had been baptized, some having been baptized in every church of the Association. Fifteen baptisms in Alarka, sixteen in Buffalo, fourteen in Cheoah, seventeen in Cold Spring, indicated where the principal revivals had been held.

Death had removed the note worthy Deacon of Stecoah, J. C. Owenby, who died in June at the age of 47 years, having lived a consistent member of the church 19 years. Nine others had obeyed the summons of death. Received by letter 34; Dismissed 47; Excluded 21; Restored 5. Total 577, net gain 94 during the year. Finance for printing minutes $14.75, quite small we see.

The dismission of Murphy church at the session of 1871 took on ordained ministers from the Association, Jesse Corn, but during the year 1872, or between the sessions of 1871 and 1872, the body had gained three more ministers. J. M. Smiley had been ordained in July, and I. T. S. Sherrill and Young Ammons had become members of the body. The Indian church had a minister by the name of Young Wolf and the ministers previously belonging were, A. Ammons, R. M. Roberts, James McBrayer and Wiley Philips.

Licentiates—G. W. Hooper. B. L. Morgan, J. R. Edwards, John Hurst and J. I. Foster.

Holly Spring and Forney's Creek churches had been organized and Refuge, a name given to an old church known as Deep Creek which had been revived, was also added to the Association.

Holly Spring had been built by the labors of R. M. Roberts, by taking greater part of Alarka membership in connection with a number of new converts in the neighborhood of Kirkland's Creek and a few others. In fact, Alarka was the mother of Holly Spring, but in truth it must be recorded that the life of the daughter was the death of the mother. Holly Spring was organized October 7, 1871 by Elders J. M. Smiley and R. M. Roberts with twenty members to which several more were soon added by letter, etc.

A good pioneer work had been done in the new settlement of Forney's Creek by Elder J. M. Smiley where he had labored for perhaps three years before his ordination, and in February 1872, Elders A. A. Justice and J. M. Smiley constituted a church which was named Forney's Creek, the name it still bears.

Strange to say that even with the gain of those three churches, Refuge. Holly Spring and Forney's Creek. there was a fall off of 44 in membership of the Association, the total being 533 members.

There had been but thirty-three baptized in the whole Association,

Panther Creek leading with the number of ten by baptism. Cold Spring with eight baptisms comes next. Buffalo and Tennessee River five baptisms each; Forney's Creek three, and Valley River two baptisms.

Fifty had been added to all the churches by letter, seven restored, sixty dismissed, ten excluded and five died.

The Association met in the eleventh anniversary with Tennessee River church, August 30th 1872. Introductory by Elder W Philips from Rev. 15; and latter clause of third verse. A. Ammons was Moderator and John S. Smiley. Clerk.

Messengers from the churches were A. Ammons, J. R. Edwards, T. L. Wikle, Brush Creek; Corn Silk, J. Cheah, Long Bear, John Tahquit-chee, Buffalo; G. W. Hooper, J. Davis, J. G. Brooks, L. Farr, W. Davis, W. Carpenter, Cheoah; J. M. Smiley, J. S. Smiley, L. L. Thomasson, N. J. Howard, J. A. Lequire, Cold Spring; Young Ammons, W. Proctor, J. W. Bradshaw, W. Mashburn, Panther Creek; M A Crisp, W. D. Crisp, J. L. Crisp. Stecoah; John Hyde, David Welch, W. F. Whiteside, P. Crisp, Tennessee River; W. Philips, James McBrayer, R. A. Bradley, Valley River. Letter sent from Valley Town. James Baird, A Watkins, W. H. Cathey, Refuge; W. J. Kimsey, S. M. B Whiteside, J. I. Foster, Holly Spring; John Hurst and James Buchanan, Forney's Creek.

Messengers from Associations were P. R. Rickman, J. D. Franks and H. J. Beck, Tuckaseige; David Owl from Notley and Revs. T. A. Ballard, Jesse Corn from Ducktown.

Committees were T. A. Bell J. M. McBrayer, H. J. Beck—Arrangements.

J. Davis, J. L. Crisp—Preaching.

T. A. Bell, J. D. Franks. W. Carpenter—Sunday Schools.

W. Philips, J. G. Brooks, J. I. Foster— Obituaries and Changes.

W D. Crisp and W. Carpenter—To write Corresponding Letters.

W. H. Cathey and William Davis—Finance.

J. M. Smiley, W. Philips, J. G. Brooks—Ministers Names and Addresses.

The first missionary effort was made at this session. The move in this direction had its origin in the report of the Sunday School Committee who reccommended the appointment of a Sunday School missionary to preach in the bounds of the Association. The choice of a missionary fell on Elder A. Ammons and an Executive Committee was appointed to fix his salary and settle with him quarterly.

Notably among the five deaths reported was sister Elizabeth Smiley who died October 7th 1871, in the 75th year of her age, having lived a consistent member of the Baptist church for fifty years. She belonged to Cold Spring at the time of her death.

Sister Mary Whitaker, wife of James Whitaker, Sr., of Valley River, had died March 20th 1872, at the advanced age of 93 years and 9 days, having been a member of the Baptist church for 66 years.

Old Father James Whitaker, Sr., had fallen from the ranks of his Valley River brethren, Nov. 2nd 1871, at the advanced age of 92 years and seven months.

Samuel Castile who by his peculiar doctrine had sown schism in some churches was denounced as an imposter. Also John H. Morgan was noticed as a false minister. Castile will be noticed farther on in this work.

Chapter VII, 1873.

Sad day for some of the Baptist churches, that Sam Castile ever pretended to preach in this part of the land. As stated in regard to Lufty church, grievous troubles had arisen by Castile's cause. Some people went so far as to believe Castile a kind of Second Christ. The evil seeds sown by him greatly injured Lufty church and two or three others in the Tuckaseige Association. He made several efforts in the Valley River, but fortunately for the good cause of truth, none of the Valley River churches, belonging to the Association at the time, were led off by Castile.

The bold and faithful Allen Ammons met Castile at Cheoah church on one occasion and so discomfitted him that he never again visited the bounds of the Association. Castile's evil influence, extended by his person, cover from February or March, 1872, to 1874 or 1875.

Castile gathered disciples and several followed him from place to place, but it is with due credit to the Baptist ministers that it may truly be said that none of them fell in with Castile, mighty as he pretended to be.

The Associational year, 1873, was rather a stand still in the ranks of the churches. The roll of Churches in the Association contained thirteen, but Alarka was dead and Forney's Creek was not represented. Valley Town church had died and been resurrected and joined the Association under the new name of Second Valley River.

This church after entertaining the Association well, asked for a letter of dismission and joined the Ducktown Association, thus leaving but one church (Valley River) in Cherokee Co. in our bounds.

While the churches had not gained much, they had held their

ground. There had bean ten baptisms in all the churches, five in Cheoah, one in Panther Creek, one in Valley River and three in Second Valley River.

Forty-six received by letter, four restored, thirty-one dismissed' fifteen excluded and eight died during the year, leaving a total, exclusive of Forney's Creek, of 532, was the rusult of the year.

The Missionary, Elder A. Ammons, had labored 159 days; traveled 725 miles; preached 180 sermons; delivered 55 lectures on Sunday Schools; organized 9 Sunday Schools, and was paid $92.45, leaving $66.55 due him at the end of the year.

M. Ghormley had moved into the Association and joined Cheoh as an ordained minister from Tennessee, making the number of ordained preachers eight. The Licentiates numbered seven

The meeting of the Twelfth Session was small in attendance. From Brush Creek—A. Ammons, J. R. Edwards; Buffalo—Corn Silk, Te-tal-e-toga; Michael Ghormley, G. W. Hooper, W. Carpenter, L. Farr, W. B. Wiggins—Cheoah; I. T. S. Sherrill, J. M. Smiley, N. J. Howard, A. H. Welch, J. P, Panther, J. S. Smiley—Cold Spring; J. L. Crisp—Stecoah; John Hyde and John M. Crisp— Tennessee River; Wiley Philips, Ute Hyatt, D. S. Puett and James Whitaker, Jr.—Valley River; W. J. Kimsey—Holly Spring. Panther Creek and Deep Creek, the latter church formerly called Refuge, were represented by letters. Messengers from sister Associations were Rev. T. A. Higdon from Ducktown, and J. L. Haynes and J. C. Sanderson from Hiwassee.

The body met with Second Valley church, September 5. Introductory by Elder J. M. Smiley from Titus 2:14. A. Ammons was Moderator and John S. Smiley, Clerk. The committees were T. A. Higdon, M. Ghormley, Ute Hyatt—Arrangements. James Whitaker, L. Farr, J. A. Kimsey—Preaching. M. Ghormly, W. Philips, J. M. Smiley—Sunday Schools. G. W. Hooper, A. H. Welch—Changes. William Carpenter, to write Corresponding Letters to sister Associations. Wiley Philips, N. N. Hyatt—Finance. Correspondence with sister Associations was appointed as usual.

At this session, the body made its first cry out against Intemperance by appointing a Committe on Temperance, Elders T. A. Higdon, M. Ghormley and J. L. Haynes, being the committee. Strong grounds were taken in regard to abstaining from all appearance of evil, and the churches advised to execute the law of Jesus Christ and to keep themselves unspotted from the world. Of course, it is not to be understood that the churches endorsed drunkenness prior to this meeting, but the first Association move, speaking out against the evil, was made here.

A Query was sent to the Association by Second Valley River church as follows:

"Where is the Scriptural attachment of the word "Rev." to Ministers' names? or, what rank does it confer?" The committe on this, viz: T. A. Higdon and G. W. Hooper, answered this: "There is no Scriptural authority for the word "Rev." to Ministers' names; but it is a term expressing veneration, and does not improperly represent a divine teacher in word and doctrine."

Four White and four Indian members died during the year. William Crisp, Sr., of Stecoah church, Jacob Davis, of Cheoah, B. L. Sawyer, of Tennessee River, and Elizabeth Jones, of Cold Spring. Perhaps no man, not a minister, was missed more than brother Jacob Davis, of Cheoah, except James Whitaker, Sr., of Valley River church.

No mission work was attempted for the ensuing year of 1874, and the body closed its labors to meet the next year, 1874, with Cold Spring church.

Nothing in the way of finance had been raised save a small minute fund.

The Association met in its thirteenth annual session with Cold Spring church, Sept. 4th, 1874. A Ammons preached the Introductory from Eph. 4:1-5.

Messengers from the churches were A. Ammons, J. M. Thomasson, William Grant, J. M. Edwards and J. S. Tabor from Brush Creek. Joshua Gibson, William Carpenter, John R. Davis and W. C. Morgan from Cheoah. J. M. Smiley, I. T. S. Sherrill. L. L. Thomasson, A.

.W. Davis, S. D. Davis, and E. M. Welch from Co:d Spring. Your Ammons, J. L. Proctor, B. L. Morgan and William Proctor fro Panther Creek. J. L. Crisp from Stecoah. David Welch, J. H. M Crisp from Tennessee River. James Whitaker, W. Philips and I W. Adams from Valley River. R. M. Roberts, W. H. Cathey, an William Whiteside from Holly Spring. Wesley Williams, T. I Chambers, J. B. Hoyle and W. B. Cole from Forneys Creek. Buffa and Deep Creek were not represented. Indian Creek church joine at this session and its messengers were, W. J. Kimsey, E. N. Bumga ner and James Baird.

Indian Creek, a new church in a pioneer settlement was built u by God's blessing, by the labors of Elder J. M. Smiley. This churc was constituted in February, 1874, by Elders J. M. Smiley and We ley Williams. Elder Williams had, but a short time before thi come into the country and joined Forney's Creek church. India Creek church commenced with eighteen members.

Messengers from sister Associations were W. H. Truitt from Hiwa see; Elder E. D. Brendle, J. D. Franks and J. S. Conner from Tuc aseige.

A. Ammons was Moderator and J. M. Thomasson, Clerk. Th Committees were W Williams, E. D. Brendle, W. H. Cathey and D. Franks—Arrangements.

Joshua Gibson, A. W. Davis, and James Whitaker—Preaching.

W. Philips, William Proctor and W. B. Cole—Sunday Schools.

R M. Roberts, T. B. Chambers, R. W. Adams—Changes.

Corresponding Letters—W. Carpenter and T. B. Chambers.

Finance—J. M. Smiley and L. L. Thomasson.

There had been but two Sunday schools in operation during th year and those were in the new churches of Forney's Creek and In dian Creek, each having one school each with three teachers and thirt pupils.

J. L. Proctor, of Panther Creek, and J. L. Crisp, of Stecoah, ha been ordained to the ministry, which with the coming in of Elde Williams from West Florida Baptist Association increased the ordai ed ministers to nine.

Alarka church had been dissolved by a presbytery during the year. Brother Pendleton Crisp, of Tennessee River; J. E. Chambers and Caroline Jenkins and Elizabeth Sumpter, of Stecoah, and Sarah Breedlove, of Brush Creek had died and passed away since last Association.

This query from Valley River church, "Is there any scriptural authority for churches to authorize a deacon to administer the ordinance of baptism; and is such baptism valid?"

The query was answered, "No."

At this session, on Sunday, the first collection for missions was taken to be applied to Home Mission purposes—collection $8.00, and a delegation collection of $2, making $10. This was the first step for representation in the Western North Carolina Baptist Convention. Elders A. Ammons and W. Williams being chosen as the first delegation from the Association to that body. Elder John Ammons, of French Broad Baptist Association was present as a transient minister and rendered valuable assistance on Sunday and Monday. Thirty-six had been baptzed, 19 of them being in Forney's Creek where a precious rrvival had been held, 18 received by letter, 4 restored, 43 dismissed, 22 excluded and five died, leaving the total membership of the Association at 451, exclusive of the churches of Buffalo and Deep Creek from which there were no reports to this session.

The year 1875 was more prosperous than the preceding one. There had been forty-eight baptisms, Brush Creek leading the van in the number baptized. Thirteen baptisms in Brush Creek church, ten in Tennessee River, seven in Holly Spring, five in Cold Spring, three in Forney's Creek, six in Indian Creek, two in Stecoah and two in Buffalo.

Sixteen had been excluded and five restored. There had been considerable changes in the churches by receiving and dismissing by letter, but we will not enter into detail of these.

Death had removed eight members from the shores of time. Sister

Mary Ammons, of Panther Creek, Jasper Kimsey, Indian Creek, Nancy Loven, Stecoah, Sister Memette, Valley River, and William Davis, of Cheoah, who was a very notable brother. Three of the Cherokees had died.

The ministerial list had been increased by the ordination of three ministers: B. L. Morgan, of Panther Creek, W. C. Morgan, of Cheoah, and an Indian brother, Armstrong Cornsilk.

Elders R. M. Roberts, of Holly Spring, and M. Ghormley, of Cheoah, were holding letters of dismission, for what reasons not known.

Two new churches had been organized during the year: Wesser Creek and Traveling Zion, the former with twenty-four members and the latter with seventeen. Wesser Creek was organized by Elders ———————————— presbytery, and Traveling Zion by Elders Crisp and Proctor, so we suppose. This little body was dismissed and moved in a body to Kansas. It was short lived and its pastor, J. L. Proctor, and the other members were scattered, some joining western churches and some returning, in a few years, to this country again. The most notable of those who returned were old Louis Medlin and wife, Jane, William Proctor and son, J. L. Proctor.

The total membership of the Association for 1875 was five hundred and sixty-one, which showed a solid advance in strength.

Elder Wesley Williams had served as missionary of the Association for 1874 which was not accounted for in the records of that year. He had served in the same capacity for 1875 with the following results:

Travelled 180 days, 1150 miles, preached 145 sermons, received 36 persons into the church, aided in ordaining three Deacons and one minister, for which he had been paid $138. Only one Sunday school was reported to the Association and that was from Cold Spring church with four officers and teachers and 110 students. Valley River, as was obtained from delegates had had two Sunday schools and Indian Creek one. It was a practice in some of the Sunday schools in those years to commit verses of Scripture to memory. The school at Panther Creek on a previous year had committed over five thousand verses in is way and the school at Cold Spring for 1875, had committed 3970 rses.

The Association made Elder Williams their Missionary and a Sab-.th collection was taken for him amounting to $8.50.

The body adopted an able Circular Letter by Elder Williams, on e subject, "Some plain reasons why we are Missionaries," which ›ubtless added new zeal to the cause in the Association.

Elders A. Ammons, J. L. Crisp and W. Williams were chosen as essengers or delegates to the Western Baptist Convention which et in Hendersonville, N. C., in September. Thursday before 4th ıbbath. Also one delegate was appointed from each church in the ssociation.

The Association met Sept. 2nd. and over its deliberations Elder mmons was Moderotor and L. M. Medlin, Clerk. Cheoah was the ace of meeting

Elder Williams preached the Introductory from the 60th Psalm ıd Eph. 4:5.

The following were the messengers from the churches:

A. Ammons, J. M. Thomasson, ?. J. Freeman, Brush Creek; 'aheyahneeta, Armstrong, Cornsilk, Thomas Bigmeat, Cornsilk and acob Cheah (Indians) from Buffalo; W. C. Morgan, G. W. Hooper, saac Carringer, J G. Brooks, William Carpenter, J. M. Davis, Louis arr, J. P Ammons from Cheoah; J. M. Smiley, ?. T. Sherrill, L. . Thomasson, H. A. Cunningham, Wm. C. Hamrick, from Cold pring; John Wiggins. A. Wiggins, from Holly Spring. A. Parris nd James Beard from Indian Creek; W. Williams, W. B. Cole. A. . Parris and Samuel Buchanan, Young Ammons, T. Y. Ammons, . L. Morgan, Wm. Mashburn, from Panther Creek, J. L. Crisp, L. I. Medlin from Stecoah; John Jenkins, W. F. Whiteside, B. J. Delozier, John Hyde, Tennessee River.; W. Philips, R. A. Bradley, . W. Adams. James Whitaker, Valley River; Thomas Wiggins om Deep Creek; J. R. Edwards, J. M. Edwards, J. N. Truitt, from Vesser Creek; J. L. Proctor, William Proctor, Louis Medlin, Travelling Zion ; Messengers from sister Associations : P. G. Green, Ammons and P. R. Rickman from Tuckaseige.

Committees were appointed on Arrangements, Preaching, Sa Schools, Changes, Digest and to write Corresponding Letters.

CHAPTER VIII. 1876.

The year, 1876, was made sad, owing to the loss of two of our worthy ministers by death. Elder Wesley Williams died March 25th, and Elder J. L. Crisp died May 1st, 1876. By the death of Elder Williams the place of Association Missionary, and the pastorates of Forney's Creek, Cold Spring and Tennessee River churches were all made vacant. None but those who knew the eminent piety, devoted zeal and characteristic kindness of Elder Crisp, could truly realize the great loss of such a man to the Baptists of the Association. Such was the feeling and esteem for Elder Williams, by Cold Spring church, that she at once appointed M. DeHart and John S. Smiley to act in concert with a committee of Forney's Creek church in getting up a sketch of his life which was promptly done.

The Association appointed a Committee at this session to sketch the life of brother John L. Crisp, which was done and reported and printed in the minutes in 1877.

Sisters Milsaps and Kirkland, of Cheoah, three brethren of Buffalo, (the Indian church,) James M. Buchanan, of Forney's Creek, and the devoted wife of Elder I. T. S. Sherrill, Sister Caroline Sherrill, had all left the church militant and were sleeping in the dust. There had been baptisms, more or less, in six of the churches, Brush Creek, Cheoah, Cold Spring, Forney's Creek, Stecoah and Wesser Creek, numbering in all, fifty-three Of the number baptized, forty-one were in Cold Spring where the most glorious series of revivals had been during the months of July and August.

Thirty-eight had been received by letter, thirty-four dismissed, nine excluded and twelve restored to fellowship in all the churches, with a total membership, exclusive of Deep Creek and Holly Spring churches which were not represented at this session, of 532.

There had been very flourishing Sunday Schools during the Spring and Summer of this year. A Sunday school at Cold Spring had ten officers and teachers and 150 persons on its roll, among whom there had been thirty conversions to God. Forney's Creek had a school with six officers and teachers and 72 pupils. Tennessee River had two good schools with 100 pupils, and two other Sunday schools made up the list for the year, being less than half the churches engaged in this good work.

The Missionary, Elder W. Williams, had only labored six months of the year at his death with the following results:

Labored 161 days; preached 55 sermons; traveled 478 miles; paid $52.40. J. M. Smiley and R. M. Roberts were delegates to the Western Convention of North Carolina

No attempt to do anything for the Foreign Mission work has yet been.

The Fifteenth Anniversary met with Forney's Creek church Thursday, August 31st. Elder Allen Ammons preached the Introductory from 1 Cor. 15:58. A. Ammons was Moderator and James M. Thomasson, Clerk.

The first effort to preserve and get up the history of the Valley River Association was made at this session by electing John S. Smiley the first Historian, by whom the work was commenced in January, 1877.

Valuable aid and encouragement was rendered at this session by the only Corresponding messengers Elders E. D. Brendle, Wilson Ensley, J. L. Buchanan, P. G. Green and brethren H. J. Beck and Philip Dills from Tuckaseige Baptist Association.

Elders A. Ammons and M. Ghormley had been appointed missionaries in the bounds of the Association, but brother Ghormley did not labor any in the work. Elder P. G. Green fills the position and by him and Elder Ammons some of the most noted revivals had been held during the year.

One hundred and sixty-two had been baptized in eight of the churches:—seven in Brush Creek, five in Buffalo, fifty-seven in Cheoah, twenty in Cold Spring, two in Holly Spring, eleven in Indian Creek, fifty-three in Stecoah and seven in Valley River. God had most signally blessed the labors of the missionaries in connection with the labors of the several pastors and a great ingathering of precious souls followed, exceeding anything that had preceded in the Association.

Forty received by letter, sixty-seven dismissed, seventeen excluded, thirteen restored and eleven died in all the churches, leaving a total of 701.

The hopeful promise and growing strength inspired the Association with new zeal and determination at the session of 1877, by which it was led to undertake the establishment of an Association High School which was subsequently located and put into operation at Stecoah church.

Committees on Education and Periodicals were raised to report on those important questions which was the first move of the kind in the Association.

The report of the Committee on education gave rise to the establishment of the High School, and the committee on Periodicals recommended the *Biblical Recorder* and *Kind Words* as there was no Baptist paper in the Western N. C. Convention at the time.

John S. Smiley and J. M. Salts were made delegates to the Western N. C. Convention.

John S. Smiley reported and was continued Historian.

The Sunday school work had gone backward, as but three schools had been in operation in the bounds, and only the one at Cold Spring church with ten officers and teachers and 101 students was truly reported.

Elders James Salts from Sevier county Tennessee, and P. G. Green, of Tuckaseige Association, had moved into the bounds. Elder M. Ghormley had taken a letter from his church and moved into the bounds of Ducktown Association, and so the ordained Ministers' list stood at 10 at the end of this year.

The death list stood thus: Sisters Nancy A. Johnson and H. A. Crisp, of Stecoah, David Welch, J. J. Calhoun, Elizabeth Cable, Hanah Crawford, of Tennessee River, W. P. Stanberry, of Cold Spring, Tom Bignett, Caroline Cornsilk, Caroline Weosisk and Noka of Buffalo

The following query from Valley River church gave rise to the appointment of a Committee on Temperance:

"Is it right tor members of Baptist churches to engage in the sale of spirituous liquors of any kind for profit?" This was answered with an emphatic "No." Correspondence was appointed to neighboring sister Associations as usual.

Able and worthy corresponding messengers, E. D. Brendle. B. N. Queen, Phillip Dills, M. L. Bradley and W. F. Potts were present from Tuckaseige Association. The delegates of Forney's Creek church were not received as she was out of order.

The sixteenth session of the Association was held with Stecoah church, Graham county, N. C., commencing Thursday, Aug. 30th, 1878.

J. M. Salts preached the Introductory from Rev. 17:14. A. Ammons was continued Moderator and the active, young brother, Thomas A. Carpenter, was for the first time. chosen Clerk. Tuckaseige church having thirteen members, organized during the year by P. G. Green and others, joined the body at this session.

The Association met in the seventeenth session with Valley River church Aug. 29th, 1878. Opening sermon by Elder A. Ammons from Math. 16:18.

A. Ammons was Moderator and W. D. Crisp, Clerk, this being brother Crisp's first term.

Twelve of the churches were represented by Messengers, Deep Creek being a blank.

Forney's Creek which was out of order at the last session had recovered from her troubles and her Messengers, W. B. Cole and T. B. Chambers, are in this session.

The little church, Wesser Creek, comes in under the name of Nantahala.

There had been two missionaries in the field in the bounds of the Association. We are unable to give any account of results, except from Elder P. G. Green. He had labored 46 days, traveled 120 miles, baptized 36, witnessed 52 conversions, preached 31 sermons and made 20 exhortations.

Elder C. M. Greene was now a member of the Association, being a messenger from Cheoah church. J. R. Edwards, of Brush Creek, and J. P. Edwards, of Tuskeegee, had been ordained to the ministry.

Sabbath schools had been on the increase in the bounds, but several of the churches had not participated in the work.

The baptisms and other statistics of the churches cannot be given for lack of the table for this year.

The world of immortality had taken possession of eleven members during the year. Isaac Rowen, Elizabeth Rodgers, and Mary Milsaps, of Cheoah, Sarah Buchanan, Margaret Buchanan, and Sarah Hagle, of Forney's Creek, Martin Whiteside, of Holly Spring, Melviney Whiteside and Nancy Marcus, of Tennessee River, Caroline Cody, of Stecoah, Deacon W. H. Cathey, of Cold Spring, were sleeping the death sleep.

The Education Board, A. Ammons, William Carpenter, James Beard and W. H. Cathey, appointed the last year reported progress on a school house for the Association High School at Stecoah church.

John S. Smiley, Historian, sent in his resignation and T. A. Carpenter was appointed to succeed him. A query was sent to the Association by Valley River church as follows: "What ought to be done with a Deacon who neither possesses the qualifications, nor practices the duties, of a Deacon as laid down in the new Testament?" The substance of the answer to this query was, admonish him to read Paul's letters to Timothy and Titus, and if such Deacons will not try to inform themselves in regard to their duties, let them be put out of office and others appointed in their places.

A Committee was appointed at this session to separate the Constitution and Rules of Order, viz: C. M Green, W. D. Crisp and T. A. Carpenter, and by resolution Mill's Parliamentary Practice was adopted as our Rules of order on points of parliamentary usage for our future guidance, thus obviating the necessity for these items under what had hitherto been called Rules of Decorum.

Union Districts were instructed to appoint Union Meetings at suitable places, and to get up subjects of importance for the benefit of young ministers. Brother T. C. Bryson, from Tuckaseige, Elder E. Kimsey, J. H. Johnson, J. A. Kimsey and Willis Parker, Hiwassee, were Corresponding Messengers present at this session.

The church roll numbered fifteen with the addition of Red Marble, a new church which had been organized during the year at Red Marble Gap in Cherokee county, which presented a petition by R. M. Wright and was admitted into the Association The body was now fast gaining strength and influence among the sisterhood of Baptist Associations. Brush Creek, had baptized twenty, Cheoah three, Cold Spring four, Holly Spring fourteen, Indian Creek five, Panther Creek two. Tennessee River five, Valley River sixteen, Tuskeegee two and Buffalo one, making sixty-two in all. Thirty-six were received by letter, sixty-eight dismissed, twenty-six excluded and nine restored and eight died during the year. Precious revivals had been held in Brush Creek, Holly Spring and Valley River, judging by their members baptized.

The total membership of the churches was 797, exclusive of Deep Creek and Red Marble whose reports were not sent up to the Association.

John P. Panther, of Cold Spring, had been ordained to the ministry in July. Three Missionaries, viz: A. Ammons, P. G. Green and Charles M. Green had been in the field. Ammons had baptized seventeen, preached 15 sermons and traveled sixty miles. P. G. Green had preached thirty sermons, made twenty exhortations, witnessed forty-seven conversions and baptized twenty-four, traveled 100 miles, labored fifty days and collected $14.50. C. M. Green had labored fifteen days. William Bradshaw, of Forney's Creek, Esther Welch, of Brush Creek, Mary Collett and Jesse Taylor, of Valley River, Caroline Penley, of Stecoah, and Young Wolf and Obediah, of Buffalo, made up the list of the dead for the year. Brother Jesse Taylor was 94 years of age when he died and had been a consistent member of the church for 65 years.

The High School of the Association had been in a very satisfactory session from the 4th of February till the 25th of June, averaging over 29 daily attendants. The teaching had been done by brother W. L. Dean and V. E. Grant, of Macon county, the former as principal at a salary of $25 per month, and the latter assistant at a salary of $20 per month. Such was the interest taken in the school undertaking that Elder A. Ammons was put into the field to raise funds for its support.

The *Biblical Recorder*, Raleigh, *Baptist*, Memphis, and *Kind Words*, were all reccommended to the people as good religious papers.

The Historian, T. A. Carpenter, had nothing to report to the body only the failure of the churches to co-operate with him in getting up facts of history of the Association.

The Sunday school work had languished, and but little had been done in this work. A Sunday collection of $7.66 for missions was taken for the Association missionaries. An effort was made by Elder C. M. Green to have the Association to organize a Sunday School Convention which move was set for the November following. The Association met in its eighteenth session with Brush Creek church Oct. 4th. C. M. Green preached the Introductory from Math. 11:11. A Ammons was Moderator and W. D. Crisp, Clerk. Corresponding Messengers from Tuckaseige Association at this session were Elders E. D. Brendle, A. A. Justice, J. S. Woodard, I. T. S. Sherrill and brethren W. L. Dean, T. C. Bryson, S. M. Welch, Philip Dills, D. S. Dills, John Ammons, J. W. Rickman, J. D Franks, R. A. Hall, M. L. Rickman and others.

Chapter IX. 1880.

From some cause not fully known to the writer, Deep Creek now disappears from the list of churches, but Yellow Creek, a new church, presented a letter and petition and was received, still keeping up the list of churches to fifteen as follows:

Brush Creek, J. S. Woodward, pastor; Cheoah, W. C. Morgan, pastor; Cold Spring, pastor blank; Forney's Creek, no pastor; Holly Spring, J. M. Smiley, pastor; Indian Creek, no pastor; Nantahala, B. L. Morgan, pastor; Panther Creek, Y. Ammons, pastor; Red Marble, W. Philips, pastor; Stecoah, P. G. Green, pastor; Tennessee River, no pastor; Tuskeega, P. G. Green and J. P. Edwards, pastors; Valley River, C. M. Green, pastor; Yellow Creek, John Canaut, pastor.

The note worthy old church, Valley River, asked for a letter of dismission at this session to join the Ducktown Association and so by its loss to this body the church roll was reduced to fourteen churches.

At this same session, following the dismission of Valley River church, the Association had no further reason to retain the name, Valley River, by which it had been known since 1869, and consequently, changed the name to Tennessee River, as a more appropriate one to locate its situation.

By the dismission of Valley River, the territory of the Association was now confined to Swain and Graham counties, N. C., with the single exception of Red Marble church, which was in Cherokee county.

The list of ordained ministers had been reduced, though Elder I. T. S. Sherrill had again become a member of the body by joining Indian Creek church.

Elder Allen Ammons, who had so faithfully served the Association as Moderator in regular succession, for ten sessions, had died July 2nd, 1880. The loss of Elder Ammons was deeply felt throughout the Association. While we mourned the loss of Ammons, not without hope of our loss being his eternal gain, we were chagrined at the disgraceful conduct of Elder R. M. Roberts, of Tennessee River church. Roberts, with a letter of dismission from said church, left his worthy wife, Nettie, and eloped from the country with another woman.

Tennessee River went through the act of excluding Roberts, but the church was powerless to recover his church letter, so after an honorable membership of about 15 or so years in the Baptist church, and a useful career of over ten years in the ministry, Elder Roberts stepped down to degredation and ruin, shamefully staining his life by dishonoring his high ministerial rank and the precious cause of the Lord Jesus Christ. Like a sudden and treacherous outburst of a volcano may surprise and startle the inhabitants of its environs, so did the man Roberts shock his brethren and sisters in Zion. We weep as we pen this event and can only say. "God be merciful to the sinner, for he is in thy just hands to be rewarded according to his works."

The worthy Elder W. Philips was dismissed with Valley River church, leaving the list of ordained ministers, up to this year. as follows:

W. C. Morgan, G. W. Hooper, the latter who had been ordained in Cheoah church during the year, J. R. Edwards, J. P. Edwards, J. P. Panther, J. M. Smiley, B. L. Morgan, I. T. S Sherrill, Y. Ammons, P. G. Green and J. M. Salts. Only five Sunday schools had been in operation during the year. There had been sixty-six baptized in ten of the churches, Yellow Creek having twenty-one, the greatest number of any Thirty had been excluded and seven restored and ten died in all the churches. The aged. sweet singer, William R. Simonds, of Brush Creek, was among the number of the dead. He was about 75 years old and had taught the young to sing the sweet songs of Zion for 52 years as a teacher of vocal music.

William Owens and Margaret Gibby, of Cold Spring, Mary and

Dinah Truitt, of Valley River, Mary Calhoun, of Tuskeega, and three Indians, of Buffalo, had all died.

One very striking feature of the year, 1880, was the work of the Missionary, Elder P. G. Green, who had labored 115 days, traveled 500 miles, preached 106 sermons, made 28 exhortations, witnessed 66 professions, baptized 53 persons, received 8 by letter, attended the ordination of 4 Deacons, attended 11 prayer meetings, orgaaized 2 Sunday schools and only received $15.50 for all this work.

Over $20 was raised among the delegates at this meeting to help brother Green.

At this session, was finally amended the Constitution, and it appeared in the minutes under the heading "CONSTITUTION OF THE TENNESSEE RIVER BAPTIST ASSOCIATION." It is a very short instrument, containing only ten articles which we will give in "*A Miscellaneous Supplement.*"

The Rules of Decorum, or Rules of Order had been previously committed to the system of Mell's Parliamentary Practice, thus obviating the necessity for so many Decorum rules attached to the Constitution.

The Association met in its nineteenth Anniversary with Tennessee River church, Thursday, Sept. 2nd.

Elder William C. Morgan preached the Introductory from Rom. 1:16.

Elder P. G. Green was Moderator and W. D. Crisp, Clerk.

As the new Constitution provided for the offices of Treasurer and Historian, those places were filled by choosing Joel L. Crisp, for the former and T. A. Carpenter for the latter.

Elder J. S. Woodard, G. W. Landersmilk and J. A. Franks were Messengers from Tuckaseige Association and rendered valuable aid to the Tennessee River Association. So ends the events of the year 1880.

Notwithstanding the dismission of Valley River church, the Association, in 1881, was rapidly approaching a higher degree of intelligence, strength and development. The twentieth Session met with

'old Spring church, Sept. 1st. The Introductory sermon was preach-
d by Elder I T. S. Sherrill from Math. 18:10.

J. M. Smiley was Moderator and W. D. Crisp, Clerk. Nothing is hown touching the Treasurer and Historian.

Tallulah, Maple Spring and Hazel Creek, three new churches had een constituted, and presented letters and messengers and were received into the Association at this session. Messengers from Tuckaeige Association as follows: Elder John S. Smiley, A. A. Justice, . D. Franks, J. A. Franks, D. K. Collins, J. M. Welch and A. W. 'armer. A beautiful sketch of the life of Elder A. Ammons was ead and adopted and will appear in Biographical Department.

A lament was made in the education report because the High School at Stecoah was doing nothing at present, but advice was given ur people to patronize Judson College. Strong grounds were taken n favor of patronizing the *Baptist Telescope*, an able Baptist paper ublished by Elder N. Bowen in Hendersonville, N. C., and also the rgan of the Western N. C. Baptist Convention.

The Mission work had been carried on part of the time the past 'ear by Elder W. C. Morgan with results as follows:

Days labored 57; miles travelled 387; sermons preached 45; exhortations 7; conversions witnessed 33; baptized 16 persons; assisted in rdaining 3 ministers and 4 deacons; constituted 1 church and 4 Sunday Schools, and had been paid $21.25.

There had been but five Sunday schools in the bounds.

It was at this session that the first efforts were made toward aiding Foreign Missions This was at the instance of Elder P. G. Green. A Sabbath collection was ordered to be applied to this purpose. The collection was $8.34. Elders P. G. Green and I. T. S. Sherrill were chosen delegates to the Western N. C. Baptist Convention.

There had been baptisms in ten of the churches numbering in all '2. It seemed that revivals had been held in Cheoah and Tahlulah hurches as 18 had been baptized in the former and 16 in the latter. Stecoah also had baptized 17 persons. Nineteen had been excluded and five restored. Ten had died and the total. exclusive of Buffalo and Nantahala was 705.

The devoted wife of Elder J. P. Panther, Charlotte E, James Buchanan, of Forney's Creek, and some others, had died.

The reports of the various Committees and the speeches following those of Mission Education, Periodicals etc. indicated a forward movement.

CHAPTER X, 1882-'83.

The Association met in the twenty-first annual session with Cheoah Baptist church Sept. 8th. Introductory sermon by James Salts from Isaiah 2:2. Elder J. S. Woodard was Moderator and W. D. Crisp, Clerk.

Elder J M. Smiley had been in the field as Association Missionary with the following results: Labored 141 days, traveled 700 miles, preached 158 sermons, baptized 39 persons, witnessed 49 conversions. delivered 11 exhortations, assisted in organizing one church, organized three Sunday schools, aided in ordaining one minister and three deacons and was paid for this service $14.05. Added to this mission fund was $8 more for Elder Smiley's work.

The Association High School which had been dormant for two or three years was to be revived again with the location to be made at Cold Spring, but the effort failed and nothing was accomplished in the High School line.

The Sunday school work for the year 1882 had been more progressive than it had in any preceding year, as there had been sixteen successful schools in the bounds.

The cause of religious periodicals was urged by the committee on that subject, and the Blue Ridge *Baptist*, published by Elders D. B. Nelson and J. E. Carter, at $1 a year in Hendersonville, N. C., was recommended, as well as the Biblical *Recorder*.

Members had died during the year to the number of fourteen: William DeHart and Mary J Freeman, of Maple Spring, Elizabeth Franklin, of Holly Spring, Jason Sherrill, of Cheoah, and 9 more whose names are not given.

Three new churches had been organized, viz: Santeetlah, Double Branch, and Bone Valley, which churches joined the Association at this session, increasing the list of churches to twenty.

Elder J. L. Proctor who had previously gone west with Travelling Zion church had returned to this country and was a member of Hazel Creek church.

Fourteen of the churches had had one hundred and twelve baptisms, a greater number being in Hazel Creek than any of the others, but several of the churches had been blessed with good ingatherings in this way. Sixty-one were received by letter, sixty-seven dismissed, excluded thirteen, and restored sixteen and the total membership was now 850.

The first Foreign Mission aid was given at the session of 1882, being $8, which was ordered through the Treasury of The Western Baptist Convention to the Foreign Board at Richmond, Va., with instructions to be paid to Rev. M. T. Yeats in China.

Queries were answered as follows:

"Is it right for a pastor to advise his church to appoint a committee to labor with a sister church?" Answer—"He has the right." "Has that church the right to declare a non-fellowship against that church which would not hear the committee?" Answer—"In our judgment she has the right."

The Association met with Forney's Creek church August 25, 1883. Introductory by Elder P. G. Green from Mark 13:35. J. S. Woodard was Moderator and John S. Smiley, Clerk. This year was one of marked prosperity. Two churches were added to the body at this session, Charleston by letter from Tuckaseige Association, and Mount Zion, a new church organized April 28, 1883, by Elders J. E. Morgan, J. M. Smiley, J. P. Panther and B. L. Morgan, with twenty members from Cold Spring church.

Charleston church had its origin chiefly from Holly Spring, but some of its constituent members were from Cold Spring church and perhaps a few from the old Deep Creek members. This church was organized in the old Court House, Dec. 1877, by Elder E D. Brendle,

W. H. Conner and J. M. Smiley, and joined the Tuckaseige Baptist Association in the session held at ————————, August, 1878.

By his membership being with this church since the spring of 1878, the writer had been identified with Tuckaseige for five years.

The writer had been ordained to the ministry, Dec. 18, 1881, in Charleston church by Elders E. D. Brendle A. A. Justice, W. H. Conner, J. M. Smiley, and J. M. Salts as presbytery.

By Charleston church becoming a member of Tennessee River Association, the writer and J. M. Smiley were added to the list of ordained ministers which now numbered fourteen, viz: J. M. Smiley, J. S. Smiley, I. T. S. Sherrill, J. E. Morgan, J. P. Panther, J. R. Edwards, J. S. Woodard, Young Ammons, B. L. Morgan, J P. Edwards, P. G. Green. W. C. Morgan. G, W. Hooper, and F. M. Morgan.

Elder J. L. Proctor had been excluded from Hazel Creek church on charge of adultery, in July, 1883. The proof of Proctor's guilt was that he left his lawful wife and left the country with another woman; thus another one of the most shameful and sickening acts of disgrace was perpetrated by a man holding the high rank of a minister of Christ.

The Licentiates were J. M. Earles, Jno. Womack, J. A. Ammons, T. S. DeHart, J. M. Rickman, H. B. Grant and Jesse Hall.

Elder John E. Morgan, chosen missionary at Cheoah, in 1882, had occupied the field in the Association with an unusual degree of success. Morgan had labored 225 days, traveled 520 miles, preached 300 sermons, made 65 exhortations, witnessed 188 conversions, baptized 167 persons, aided in organizing one church and ordaining four deacons and had been paid $149.25.

There had been 181 baptisms in sixteen of the churches. Forney's Creek church had baptized 53 persons, Cold Spring 34, Mt. Zion 18, Cheoah 14, and Double Branch14. In fact there had been gracious revivals in a majority of the churches. Seventy-three had been received by letter, seventy-three dismissed, twenty-three excluded, restored 15 and 11 had died in all the churches with the great total in the Association of eleven hundred members which was a net gain during the year of 250 members. Some internal troubles in Tallulah church, caused, we suppose, by the preaching of a man by the name of Walker, resulted in that church's absence from the session of 1883, by which 45 members are not reported in our aggregate. Tallulah finally went down and is never again represented in the councils of our Association.

The Sunday School work had been successful and the importance of this cause was steadily and certainly taking hold of the churches, as there had been twenty Sunday schools in operation during the year.

The cause of Education. Temperance and Missions received a deeper impulse at this session, and very warm committee reports on these several subjects followed by enthusiastic speeches on this occasion led the brethren to believe themselves under obligations to do more for the increase of religious knowledge in this Association, and to labor more for the spread of the gospel in other lands. Brother W. M. Taylor had by request written a very forcible Circular Letter for the Association on the Duties of Churches to their Ministers, which we think had a good effect on its readers as it was adopted and printed in the minutes at this session. Brother J. C. Sorrells was elected Historian of the Association and some sketches of Elder A. Ammon's pastoral labors with Cowee church turned over to Brother Sorrells, but as he failed to make any future report this sketch was lost and nothing else accomplished by Brother Sorrells toward getting up the Association hisitory.

A stronger co-operation with the Western N. C. Convention was determined upon, and as some funds for missions had been raised, Elders J. S. Woodard, J. E. Morgan and brother Joel L. Crisp were delegated to said Convention.

Elders C. F. Weston, of Maine. A. A. Justice. W. W. Reid and P. R. Rickman, of Tuckaseige, S. F. Payne, of New Found, and J. G. Pulliam, of Buncome County Associations were present and participated in the work of the Association Correspondence was kept up with Tuckaseige and other Associations.

CHAPTER XI.

Every church in Tennessee River Association, except Tallulah, was represented. This session was held with Charleston church, commencing on Thursday, Aug. 22, 1884. J. S. Woodard preached the Introductory from Phil. 2:14. J. S. Woodard was chosen Moderator and John S. Smiley, Clerk.

The year 1884 was also a year of prosperity in the Association. Alarka, a new church with members from Cold Spring, had been organized April 26, 1884, by Elders J. E. Morgan, J. M. Siniley and J. S. Smiley as presbytery. And Tellico, also a new church with members from Burningtown church and others in which was the noted Elder A. A. Justice, was organized by Elder Justice and ———— August 2, 1884. These two presented letters and petitions and were added to the Association, making the number of churches twenty-four.

The Association was favored with the presence of Elders E. D. Brendle, W. H. Conner, A. H Sims and J. H. Queen and brethren J. D. Franks, H. J. Beck, P C. Wild, G. E. Davis, J. B. Gibson, W. H. Queen, T. C. Bryson, J. E. Hurst and H. D. Welch, of Tuckaseige Association, and J. G. Pulliam, of Buncombe county, and T. C. Buchanan and M. L. Rickman, of Central Association, N. C., and Elder James Salts, of Little River Association, Tennessee, the latter named brother, having moved out of our bounds.

A good Sunday collection for missions was made amounting to $240, twelve dollars of which was paid to Elder J. E. Morgan, Association Missionary, and twelve collars forwarded to Richmond for Mexican missions.

Elder J. E. Morgan had been kept in the field as Association Mis sionary, but he he had not been so successful as he had the previous year. He had labored 225 days, traveled 275 miles, preached 200 sermons, witnessed 71 conversions, baptized 66 persons, aided in organizing two churches; amount received for said labor $100. There had been baptisms in fifteen of the churches · twenty-eight in Tuskeega, 23 in Stecoah, 14 in Tennessee River and 10 in Bone Valley, these churches having the largest ingatherings in this way. Forty-two had been excluded, twenty-six restored and fourteen died during the year in all the churches. The total membership was now 1267.

Elder Young Ammons, of Panther Creek church, was numbered with the dead and thirteen others whose names are not given, were gone from earth.

All the churches had been blessed with faithful pastors and to the labors of these in connection with Elder Morgan, the Missionary, the Lord had given the increase and a healthy growth of the Association.

The minute fund was $20.05, and all receipts and disbursements which had found their way into the Treasury were $44.45, according to the report of the Treasurer, Joel L. Crisp.

Brother J. C. Sorrells had served the Western Convention as Sunday School Missionary and Colporteur in the bounds, but we received no report of his work.

J. P. Panther and J. M. Earls were appointed delegates to the Western Baptist Convention by this session. The churches nearly all reported the salaries of their pastors which run from 7 to fifty-eight dollars.

The twenty fourth annual session met with Double Branch church, Aug. 20, 1885. Introductory by Elder J. P. Panther, Neh. 4:6. Elder A. A. Justice was Moderator and W. D. Crisp, Clerk.

Every church was represented but Red Marble.

Three new churches were received into the Association, viz: Pleasant Grove, being a part of Forney's Creek, was constituted November 22, 1884, by Elders J. M. Smiley and John E. Morgan,

Welch Cove, constituted October 25, 1884, by Elders J. M. Smiley and John Pickney Panther; Chamber's Creek organized Feb. 21st, 1885, by Elders J. M. Smiley and L. M. Medlin, with members from Forneys Creek and Tennessee River. This year four ministers were ordained, Elder J. M. Earles, of Cold Spring, L. M. Medlin, of Bone Valley, J. A. Ammons, of Maple Spring, and C. I. Calhoun, of Double Branch.

By the foregoing, the list of churches was run up to twenty-seven and the list of ordained ministers increased to eighteen.

Elder J. P. Panther had occupied the field as Association Missionary with the following results: labored 250 days, travelled 1,500 miles, preached 275 sermons, made 200 exhortations, witnessed 28 conversions, baptized 25, organized three Sunday Schools and received on the field $80.

The body now attempted greater efforts in the mission work by creating an Association Mission Board which consisted of Elders W. C. Morgan, L. M. Medlin and brethren J. W. Breedlove, J. C. Sorrells and J. H. Sentell and $138 were pledged toward the mission work for the next year. There had been but forty-three baptisms in ten of the churches: 14 in Cold Spring, 7 in Cheoah, 9 in Panther Creek, the churches having the greater number baptized. The changes by letter had been greater than usual and the exclusions were 51 and the restorations only four. Sixteen had died and the total membership in all the churches outside of Buffalo, Red Marble and Tallulah was 1169.

Numbered among the sixteen deaths were Elder J. P. Edwards, of Tuskeegee, William Carpenter, of Cheoah, and Samuel Monteith, of Forney's Creek. While these three named were not more precious in the sight of the Lord than the other thirteen who had died, they were more greatly missed and mourned by the Association because of their notoriety and rank in the church.

Most of the churches had been engaged in the noble Christian work of Sunday Schools.

Only thirteen of the churches reported their pastor's salaries which ranged from $1 to $100.

Elder W. W. Reid, of Tuckaseige Association, and J. E. Carter, editor of the Blue Ridge *Baptist*, were present and participated in the session.

Foreign missions, Temperance, and Education and Periodicals received enthusiastic encouragement and all the Sunday collection was divided equally between Mexican and Chinese missions. Committees were appointed to prepare sketches of Elders Young Ammons and J. P. Edwards, deceased, but no report was ever made.

CHAPTER XII, 1886.

The period of organising churches in the territory or even the necessity for such was now at an end and a very prudent step had been taken by Tennessee River and Double Branch in the work of consolidation by which Double Branch is merged into her mother organization, Tennessee River church, making one strong church instead of two week ones.

The work of ordaining ministers had out-stripped any preceding year in our history.

Will Pruitt, of Cheoah; H. B. Cook, of Bone Valley; R. H. Crisp, of Tennessee River; W. A. Marcus, of Tuskeega; and J. H. Sentell, of Double Branch or Tennessee River churches had all been ordained and Elder G. W. Orr and J. H. Queen had moved into the Association, thus swelling the list of ordained ministers to twenty-three.

The Mission Board of the Association had had Elder J. E. Morgan in the field as missionary, but he had labored only forty-four days and been paid $14. Fifty-three days labor had been rendered in the mission work by Elders J. M. Earles, J. P. Panther, L. M. Medlin and T. S. DeHart. Connected with this work were 46 conversions and 22 baptisms. It seemed that the new and untried machinery of a Mission Board had not met with the necessary co-operation by the churches and pastors, notwithstanding the worthy service of such instrument.

We think, however, that much of the failure of the mission work in the Association for 1886, was attributable to Elder Morgan's services in sections of country out of the bounds. Brush Creek, Nantahala and Tallulah were not represented by messengers, but the total membership at the end of the year was 1260, exclusive of those three churches and if those churches were taken into the count there were at least 1330 members in the Association. One hundred and ten had been baptized in the bounds, Alarka 1, Buffalo 2, Cheoah 17, Cold Spring 3, Holly Spring 10, Hazel Creek 1, Indian Creek 19, Mt. Zion 8, Panther Creek 5, Santeetlah 11, Tuskeega 3, Tennessee River 11, and Welch Cove 19.

Dismissed by letter, 93 and received by letter 81. Excluded forty and restored seven.

Seventeen had died during the year, among whom were Elder I. T. S. Sherrill and John Kilby, of Indian Creek; Jane DeHart, of Cold Spring; Matilda Hooper, of Cheoah, and sister Elenor Ammons, of Panther Creek; these were much missed from the earthly sanctuary on account of their ages and long service in the Master's kingdom in the world.

Elder P. G. Green who had labored so successfully as Missionary and pastor in the bounds of the Association for a period of nine years had been excluded from Stecoah church on a charge equivalent to fornication, and, as a consequence, the Association loses a most popular preacher whose work shows a good degree of success; but oh! how mortified were the brethren and sisters generally to see the sudden downfall of such a man stained with immortal death to his Christian and ministerial character and usefulness!

The Association met with Panther Creek church, Aug. 22nd. Elder L. M. Medlin preached the Introductory from Neh. 6:3. Elder A. A. Justice was Moderator, L. M. Medlin, Clerk; J. M. Earls, Treasurer, and John S. Smiley, Historian. A standing order of business was made at this session by which the committee of Arrangements were dispensed with. The order will be found in the appendix.

The Association met in its twenty-sixth session with Indian Creek church, Thursday, August 25th, 1887. Elder A. A. Justice preached the Introductory from Math. 17:20. Elder John M. Earls presided and W. D. Crisp Clerked.

A smaller delegation than usual from the churches, being eleven or twelve churches without messengers, but much territory and efficient strength were added at this session by the joining of Lutty church by letter from Tuckaseige Association through her messengers, W. H. Queen and H. K. Gass.

W. H. Queen was chosen Treasurer and Jno S. Smiley was continued Historian.

The Association Mission Board had had Elder A. A. Justice in the field for one hundred and twenty days during the year, and had collected and paid him $86.45, which was supplemented by the Association among the messengers to $100, the amount stipulated by the Board, but what the result of Elder Justice's labors was is not given.

There had been seventy-two baptisms in nine of the churches represented, but so inaccurate and missing are the statistics given on account of so many of the churches not reporting and with the statistics credited to the wrong church, that we shall not attempt any more on that line for the year 1887.

The Association again took its mission work into hand and Elder J. A. Ammons was elected for the next year and be given the field for his salary, by which act the Association Board of Missions was practically discontinued.

Elder J. M. Earls, the retiring Treasurer, reported $8 received by him last year and the same disbursed to Elder Justice.

Missions, Temperance and all kinds of denominal work, such as are generally committed to Associations, received warm endorsement by the body, and on Sunday $12.00 for Foreign Missions were collected. By receipts for mission purposes at the rate of $5 per seat, eight messengers or delegates were appointed to go to the W. N. B. Convention, viz: J. H. Sentell, L. M. Medlin, J. S. Woodard, J. S. Smiley, S. B. Gibson, W. D. Crisp, T. M Buchanan and J. H. Queen.

Elder John E. Morgan, the successful Evangelist, had moved out of the Association and became a member of Burningtown church in Tuckaseige Association.

Elders W. W. Reid and G. W. Crawford, of Tuckaseige Association, were present as Corresponding Messengers. Corsesponding Messengers were appointed to sister Associations by a motion, authorizing any member of this Associotion who may be present at others to report as Messengers. The method of writing Corresponding letters had been discontinued for several years, which is an error in practice without a doubt from the good reason that a Christian Salutation from a sister body or church is in accord with Apostolic usage. These Corresponding letters are official certificates of the standing ot those appointed to bear such fraternal greetings and relationship and the writing of such letters should be resumed by all Associations.

By a vote, Cold Spring church was chosen as a site for the revival of the Association High School and a Board of School Trustees, to wit, H. G. Beck, J. A. Franks. S. B. Gibson, J. S. Woodard, J. S. Smiley, J. A. Ammons, L. M. Medlin and J. A. Buchanan, of Swain county, and W. D. Crisp, W. M. Taylor and W. C. Morgan, of Graham county, were appointed to endeavor to put the School in operation.

Several of the churches were not represented at the last session, owing, it was said, to a severe epidemic in Bryson City at the time of the Association, but when the body met at Stecoah church, August 23, 1888, there were about 100 messengers from the churches and all the churches were represented but Brush Creek, Nantahala, Red Marble and Hazel Creek.

A disagreement or dissatisfaction on the part of the members formerly known as Double Branch, led to a dissolution of the act of consolidation with Tennessee River church, by which Double Branch took up its former organization and record and enrolls as a church.

Red Marble, so long without representation in the Association, had been somewhat revived, as we have been informed, and inconsistently left the Association without leave, and as a consequence was dropped from the church roll.

Pleasant Grove church, by mutual agreement with its mother, Forney's Creek, had been merged into one body by the old name, and so Pleasant Grove disappeared from the church roll of the Association.

Lone Oak on Cheoah, Bethabara on Lufty, Fairview, formerly of Double Branch, and Land's Creek had all been constituted during the year and were admitted into the Association at this session.

Bethabara was organized Oct 22nd, 1887, by Elders J. M. Smiley and J. H. Queen, of members from Shoal Creek and Indian Creek churches. Welch Cove church had changed its name to Eagle Creek.

The Association year 1888 had been a year of prosperity, as there had been 140 baptisms in twenty-one of the churches, Charleston church under the successful preaching of its new pastor, Rev. G. H. Church, having baptized twenty, the largest number in any one of the churches.

Thirty-three had been excluded and eleven restored in all the churches. Receiving and dismissing by letter had gone on very extensively, and sixteen members had passed into the Spirit world, and the total membership was 1,558.

Elder G. H. Church had moved into the bounds from Transylvania County Association. Elder O. P. Williams had been ordained, thus greatly strengthening the ministry of Tennessee River Association.

The Trustees appointed at last session to start a school had employed Prof. J. S Hill, of Elk Park, Mitchell county, and had run a successful session of school for 70 days, commencing Jan. 23. The school enrolled 95 pupils and averaged 46. Mr. Hill's salary was $50 a month.

V. M. Caler had also been employed to run another session at a salary of $35 per month. Mr. Caler's school covered a period of about 7 months in connection with the free public school which finally closed the school effort for the time being. Both schools resulted in good to our people.

The Sunday school work had been kept up, there being twenty schools in the bounds. A Ministers' Council had been organized during the session at Stecoah, but the organization was not kept up. For a number of years the Union Meetings had been assembling and transacting business by their own appointments from fifth Sunday to fifth Sunday under the name, "Tennessee River Union," but without reports to the Association, so we know very little of their history.

It was very gratifying to note the zealous mission, temperance and education spirit of the session 1888. Good collections were made for missions and education, amounting in pledges and cash to $110.04.

The Association mission was suspended at this session and a Colporteur appointed to travel and sell books and furnish Scriptures and religious literature to the destitute—Elder T. S. DeHart being chosen for the place.

The twenty-seventh anniversary was presided over by Elder J. A. Ammons, L. M. Medlin was Clerk, J. S. Smiley Historian and W. H. Queen was Treasurer.

Elder J. A. Ammons had occupied the field as Missionary and had labored 139 days; travelled 900 miles; preached 126 sermons; made 23 exhortations; witnessed 41 conversions; baptized 23 persons; was paid on the fie d, $123. Elder G. H. Church preached the Introductory.

The twenty-eighth session met with Lufty church Thursday, Aug. 22. John S. Smiley preached the Introductory from 1st Pet. 2:5. A. A. Justice was Moderator, E. C. Monteith, Clerk, W. H. Queen, Treasurer, and John S. Smiley, Historian. Ten of the thirty churches, composing the Association, were not represented at this session, but a more spsrited and enjoyable session had never been. Love seemed to rule the session and the subjects engaging the work of the Association received enthusiastic efforts by all.

Messengers returned to their homes praising the good Association which they had attended.

Elders A. H. Sims, M. L. Rickman and T. C. Buchanan were present as Corresponding Messengers from Tuckaseege Association and gave valuable aid in the deliberations of this session.

Elder M. Rodgers had been ordained some time previous to this session and with the addition of his name the list of ordained ministers now numbered twenty-three.

The Baptist Orphanage of the Baptist State Convention of North

Carolina, received attention at this meeting for the first time and $8.50 was raised to aid the Orphanage.

Foreign Missions received warm attention and over $80 in pledges and cash were raised for said purpose.

Elder T. S. DeHart had occupied the field as Colporteur 71 days; travelled 1,010 miles; preached 36 sermons; made 34 addresses; made 181 religious visits; attended 30 prayer meetings; witnessed 32 professions and 20 baptisms; sold 21 Bibles and 57 Testaments; sold 96 other books; value of books sold, $63.15; organized 6 Sunday schools and collected on the field on salary $8.00.

J. S. Smiley, J. S. Woodard, J. H. Queen, Wm. Pruitt, J. M. Smiley, A. A. Justice, H. J. Beck and W. D. Crisp were made Messengers to the Western North Carolina Baptist Convention.

The School at Cold Spring had been run seven and a half months under Mr. V. M. Caler as teacher, but as there was no suitable house and the co-operation being discouraging no attempt was made to run another session. A committee was appointed to build a house and about $400 previously subscribed toward that purpose, but from various discouragements nothing was done, and so there the Association School rests, in quiet repose.

Seventy persons had been baptized during the year in fourteen of the churches. J. H. Sentell had been ordained to the ministry. Sweet Water church had been constituted and joined the Association.

Sister Elizabeth Crisp, of Stecoah, who had been a devoted member of the church for forty years had died July 20, Gemima Aldredge, of Panther Creek, Catharine Woody, of Forney's Creek, H. P. Childers, of Bethabara, and some others not named, had all died during the year.

Elder G. H. Church had been prevented from attending this session on account of the death of his daughter, Laura.

One singular feature of the session of 1889 was that, no church had invited the Association for the next year, and as a consequence some of the delegations had to assume the responsibility of inviting the next session to meet with their church, and the lot fell to the Cold Spring delegation, which invitation was accepted by the Association.

The Treasurer's report for 1889, shows $14.90 for foreign missions; $7.10 for ministerial education.

The minute fund was only $18.35.

CHAPTER XIII, 1890.

The twenty-ninth Anniversary of the Association met with Cold Spring church August 21st, 1890 with ninety-nine messengers from twenty-four of her twenty-eight churches. Eagle Creek and Land's Creek disappeared from the church roll as being considered dead churches. The Introductory sermon was preached by Elder J. A. Ammons, the Alternate of Elder William Pruitt, from Math. 28:19, 20.

Elder J. S. Woodard was Moderator, E. C. Monteith, Clerk, S. B. Gibson, Treasurer, and Jno. S. Smiley, Historian.

This session was one of love and harmony throughout and was noted for the punctuality of the messengers and congregations.

All the subjects engaging the attention of the Association received patient and faithful consideration, so much so that it brought forth the eulogies of Rev. D. B. Nelson, Editor of the Asheville *Baptist*, as he was present as a visitor and witnessed the delibrations of the body.

Round Hill church, newly constituted of members from Mt. Zion church. by a presbytery of Elders J. M. Smiley and T. S. DeHart, was admitted at this session.

There had been twenty-seven Sunday schools, all the churches having Sunday schools except Cheoah, Alarka, Hazel Creek, Round Hill and Santeetlah.

There had been eighty-seven baptized in seventeen of the churches, those having the largest numbers baptized being Lone Oak with fifteen, and Stecoah with twenty. All the churches had been well supplied with pastors except Alarka, which is standing as dead or asleep.

There had been seventeen deaths during the year, viz: Laura N. Church, Bryson City; Daniel and Elijah Gibby, Cold Spring; J. A.

'hilders, Bethabara· Mary Smith, Tellico; Alfred Crisp, Stecoah; Mary 'risp,, N. J. Bradshaw and Cassie Hogue, Panther Creek; Laura Laıey, Bone Valley; James S. Tabor, Brush Creek; Sarah Skeeska, Ellz.beth Axe, Buffalo; Nancy Bumgarner and M. J. Stevenson, Indian 'reek; Israel Carver and Lavada Mathis, Lufty; Avaline Carringer, ıanteetlah; Wm. Anthony, Chamber's Creek.

Samuel Jordan, of Cheoah, had been ordained to the ministry. Elder A. B. Thomas had labored in Graham county eight months as nissionary under the appointment of the Mission Board of the W. N. '. C. with success. The Tennessee River Union was dissolved and wo unions made, viz. Swain County Union and Graham County Jnion to which the Mission work was committed.

The thirtieth Anniversary of the Association met with Cheoah hurch. As Elder G. H. Church, the appointee to preach the Introluctory, was not present, the Alternate, Elder J. H. Queen, performed he task from Rom. 1:16. Elder J. S. Woodard was continued Moderitor and E. C. Monteith, Clerk. W. H. Queen was Treasurer and 'no S. Smiley, Historian.

The year 1891 had been a prosperous one, and the life and zeal of he churches brought out a fair list of messengers to this session of the Association. Twenty-five out of the thirty churches were represented, ınd one new church had been organized, by the name Antioch out of nembers from Indian Creek church. This young church was represented ıy brethren James Cline and W. M. Clark. Elders G. H. Church and Γ. J. Brock were the presbytery that constituted Antioch.

At this session, Rev. John Ammons, Corresponding Secretary of he Convention and Rev. J. A. Speignt, editor of the Asheville *Baptist*, were present and took an active part in the deliberations. There ıad been 121 persons baptized in 18 of the churches. Brush Creek. Maple Spring, Indian Creek, Lufty and Sweet Water, had precious ingatherings to a greater extent than the others.

Death had taken nineteen members from all the churches. Among hose gone were Deacon J. M. Thomasson, who died in March 1891 a the advanced age of about 85 years, and Elder J. M. Smiley at the age of over 70 years died July 12th, 1891. Elders L. M. Medlin and J. P. Panther had moved out of the bounds of the Association; the first named had settled in Jackson county, N C

A standstill in the growth of the Sunday School cause were the results of the year. Twenty-two schools, numbering 1280 pupils had been in operation, a fall off of 5 schools from the previous year.

The Association had done nothing in the line of Home Missions but continued its friendly co-operation with the mission work of the world.

The session for 1892, met with Forney's Creek church, Aug. 25th. and was in session four days. The usual committees were appointed after the organization of the session was effected. Elder Woodard was Moderator and brother A. J. Hall, Clerk. Six out of the 30 churches were not represented, but a very large delegation attended.

Jesse R. Starnes, president of Judson College and Rev. J. A. Speight, editor of the Asheville *Baptist* were present.

A forward movement in good works had resulted in a hundred and twenty-seven additions by baptism, but more exclusions than usual in all the churches aggregating thirty-six. Fourteen churches had been blessed with revivals and nineteen had reported baptisms. Twenty-seven Sunday Schools numbering, 1232 students had been in operation. Several of the pastors had been active in the revival work. Elder J. M. Earles, with the pastor, G. H. Church, of Bryso City church, had baptized 19. Elder Justice at Maple Spring had baptized 23. Elders Woodard and Pruitt and most of the pastors had good success in their charges.

No Associational Missionary had been in the field for the year.

Nineteen dear brethren and sisters had died out of ten of the churches. Brother J. C. Holoway, of Cheoah was among the number of the deceased.

Rock Spring, an Indian church, newly constituted, joined the Association, but Fair View church had been consolidated with Double Branch and so disappeared from the church roll; so the church roll ending with August, 1892, stands as follows: Antioch, Alarka, Brush Creek, Buffalo, Bone Valley, Bethabara, Bryson City, Cheoah, Cold Spring, Chambers Creek, Double Branch, Forney's Creek, Holly Spring, Hazel Creek, Indian Creek, Lufty, Lone Oak, Maple Spring, Mt. Zion, Nantahala, Panther Creek, Round Hill, Rock Spring, Stecoah, Santeetlah, Sweet Water, Tuskeega, Tennessee River, Tellico, Qellow Creek, all numbering a total of about 1000 members in Swain county and about six hundred in Graham. But little had been done for missions, but the State Baptist Orphanage had been aided.

An attempt was made to revive the Association High School by locating it at Bayson City, but it failed. An effort was made to start a High School by the joint co-operation of Tuckaseige, Tennessee River and Western N. C. Associations by committees appointed in August at the sessions which is yet an experiment to result in success we hope.

Four ministers had been ordained J. W. Justice, of Tellico, in December 1891; H. H. Hyde, of Mt. Zion; H. A. Cunningham, of Cold Spring in May 1892, and W. C. Hamrick, of Nantahala in June, 1892.

List of ministers and officers as follows:

OFFICERS OF THE ASSOCIATION AND THEIR POSTOFFICES.

J. S. Woodard, Moderator, Needmore, N. C. A. J. Hall, Clerk, Wayside; W. H. Queen, Treasurer, Lufta; J. S. Smiley, Historian, Swain.

MINISTERS' NAMES.

G. H. Church, Bryson City, J. H. Queen, Bryson City; J. M. Earles, Bryson City; J. S. Smiley, Swain; T. S. DeHart, Swain; J. R. Edwards, Swain; H. A. Cunningham, Swain; H. H. Hyde, Swain; J. S. Woodard, Needmore; J. A. Ammons, Needmore; B. L. Morgan, Welch; A. A. Justice, Etna; J. W. Justice, Etna; R. H. Crisp, Dorsey; M. Rogers, Dorsey; C. T. Calhoun, Wayside; John Jackson, Robbinsville; G. W. Orr, Robbinsville; G. W Hooper, Robbinsville: Wm. Pruitt, Robbinsville; O. P. Williams, Robbinsville;

S. M. Jordan, Robbinsville; W. C. Morgan, Robbinsville; W. R. Caldwell, Robbinsville; T. J. Calhoun, Medlin; H. B. Cook, Medlin; John Lester. Bushnell; W. C. Hamrick, Nantahala.

LICENTIATES.

W. Slaughter, Robbinsville, J. B. Brooks, Dorsey, J. C Laney, Wayside; A. Wiggins, Bryson City; D. S. Collie, Bryson City; W. E. Conner, Bryson City; Wm. Welch, Procter; C. Lester, Tuskegee; W. M. Chambers, Robbinsville.

HISTORICAL SUMMARY.

Now, after this Association has existed thirty-one years, we wish to give a summary of its growth. It was organized Oct. 25, 1861, with six small churches on Valley River at Valley Town church now known as Second Valley River. Once had Murphy, Valley River, Red Marble, Second Valley River in Cherokee county. The Association was known as Friendship until 1868 when the name was changed to Valley River which name it retained until 1880 when it was changed to Tennessee River. The little body gathered eastward and now covers only Swain and Graham counties with the exception of Tellico in Macon. Organized with not exceeding 300 members and now numbers 1,600.

ADDITION.

Statistics of churches gained in the Associacion since October, 1861.

In organization,	6.
New churches organized.	32.
Received by letter,	4.
Total.	42.

DIMINUTION.

Dismissed by letter,	4.
Dissolved, etc.,	8.
Total loss,	12.
Present Roll of Churches,	30.

MINISTERIAL CHANGES.

Ministers in organization of Association,	3.
Ministers added by letter,	7.
Ministers ordained,	33.
Ministers excluded,	3.
Ministers died,	8.
Present number of ordained Ministers,	30.
Licentiates,	9.
Total number,	39.

HISTORICAL TABLE---1861 TO 1890.

Years	Moderators	Clerks.	Treasurers.	Historians.	Missionaries
1861	James Kimsey	Mark May			
1862	James Whitaker	A. Taylor			
1863	The Association	did not	organize	on account	of hostile raid
1864	James Whitaker	C. N. George			
1865	James Whitaker	J. A. Kimsey			
1866	James Whitaker	J. A. Kimsey			
1867	James Kimsey	J. A. Kimsey			
1868	James Kimsey	James Whitaker			
1869	James Kimsey	James Whitaker			
187	A. Ammons	James Whitaker			
1871	A Ammons	James Whitaker			
1872	A. Ammons	J. S. Smiley			A. Ammons
1873	A. Ammons	J. S. Smiley			A. Ammons
1874	A. Ammons	J. M. Thomasson			
1875	A. Ammons	L. M. Medlin			W. Williams
1876	A. Ammons	J.M. Thomasson		J. S. Smiley	W. Williams
1877	A. Ammons	T. A. Carpanter		J. S. Smiley	A. Ammons
1878	A. Ammons	W. D. Crisp		T. A. Carpenter	P. G. Green
1879	A. Ammons	W. D. Crisp		T. A. Carpenter	P. G. Green
1880	P. G. Green	W. D. Crisp	J. L. Crisp	T. A. Carpenter	P. G. Green
1881	J. M. Smiley	W. D. Crisp	J. L. Crisp	T. A. Carpenter	W. C. Morgan
1882	J. S. Woodard	W. D. Crisp	J. L. Crisp	T. A. Carpenter	J. M. Smiley
1883	J. S. Woodard	J. S. Smiley	J. L. Crisp	J. C. Sorrells	J. E. Morgan
1884	J. S. Woodard	J. S. Smiley	J. L. Crisp	J. C. Sorrells	J. E. Morgan
1885	A. A. Justice	W. D. Crisp	J. M. Earls	J. C. Sorrells	J. E. Morgan
1886	A. A. Justice	L. M. Medlin	J. M. Earls	J. S. Smiley	T. S. DeHart
1887	J. M. Earls	W. D. Crisp	W. H. Queen	J. S. Smiley	A. A. Justice
1888	J. A. Ammons	L. M. Medlin	W. H. Queen	J. S. Smiley	J. A. Ammon,
1889	A. A. Justice	E. C. Monteith	W. H. Queen	J. S. Smiley	T. S. DeHart
1890	J. S. Woodard	E. C. Monteith	S. B. Gibson	J. S. Smiley	T. S. DeHart

HISTORICAL TABLE CONTINUED.

Years.	Baptisms	Received By Letter	Restored	Dismissed By Letter	Excluded	Died	Totals	Sunday Schools	Sunday School Pupils	Finances	
1865	3	5	3		1	2	128			$ 8	52
1866	53	20	6	33	17	1	405			20	13
1867	26	38	2	32	13	4	377			22	00
1868	30	25	4	27	19	4	465			17	80
1869	53	52	4	43	19	5	420			18	00
1870	28	27	4	26	6	8	485			23	10
1871	81	[illegible]	5	47	21	10	577			14	75
1872	33	30	7	60	10	5	533			19	30
1873	10	46	4	31	15	8	532			14	00
1874	36	18	4	43	22	5	457			12	00
1875	48	27	5	51	16	8	561			13	20
1876	53	38	12	34	9	9	532	3	350	9	30
1877	162	40	13	67	17	11	701			11	00
1878	36	40	12	60	16	11	740			10	50
1879	62	36	9	68	26	8	797			25	00
1880	66	29	7	40	30	[illegible]	824	5		11	70
1881	72	28	5	84	19	10	705	7		42	25
1882	112	61	16	67	13	14	850	16		40	90
1883	181	73	15	73	23	11	1101	20	456	184	85
1884	156	90	26	113	42	14	1267	18	759	144	55
1885	43	67	4	130	53	16	1200	15		102	00
1886	110	81	7	93	40	21	1260	15		76	45
1887	72	56	6	77	24	5	1300	18		125	00
1888	139	143	11	154	33	15	1278	21			
1889	72	85	21	85	44	7	1167	18	1161	57	55
1890	87	71	21	84	34	20	1380	26	1339	56	00
Totals	1824	1280	233	1602	581	242	1400	26	1339		

LIFE SKETCHES

OF

Over Twenty Devoted Servants

OF THE

Baptist Church in Western North Carolina,

WHOSE WORK

HAS BEEN DIRECTLY CONNECTED

WITH

TENNESSEE RIVER BAPTIST ASSOCIATION.

Elder Humphrey Posey.

Humphrey Posey was born in Henry county, Virginia, Jan 12th, 1780, when he was about five years old, his father removed Burke county, N. C., where young Posey spent his childhood. mother taught him when but a child, having no spelling book spell and read, and by the time he was seven years old, he had the New Testament through several times without having gone school more than twenty days.

His parents moved to Greenville, S. C., and when he was about enteen years old he commenced teaching what he called an " Field School." In the spring of 1799, he went into Union Distric follow the same occupation.

On the 28th day of January, 1800, he married to Miss Lettie J and taught school that year in the same community, and in 1 removed to Greenville again. On the 10th day of June, 1802, P joined the Baptist church. He was licensed to preach in 1803, an 1804 moved to Buncombe county, N. C. Cane Creek church was tablished 10th day of May, 1806, and Posey was ordained to the n istry on the same day. Elder Posey was appointed Missionary to Cherokee Indians, Nov. 24th, 1817. After leaving this work he mo to Macon county, N. C., and settled three miles below Franklin Tennessee river. Here Posey dwelt for many years until 1842, w he moved to Murray county, Ga., where his wife died.

From Murray he moved to Newnan, Ga., where he formed his ond marriage to a widow, Jane Stokes. But we wish to note Pos work in N. C., while he lived in Macon county.

About the year 1829, he with Adam Corn, organized Mt. Zion I tist church, near Arneeche Ford on Oconee Lufty, and in Dec. 1832, he and others as presbytery organized Brush Creek Baptist church on Tennessee river, about 15 miles below where Posey lived. In the latter church Posey was pastor for 1833, being the first pastor of this young organization. From these two churches have mostly sprung all the churches of Tennessee River Association. Posey would ride from his home on Saturday mornings to Brush church meetings by 11 o'clock a. m, to preach and find a shelter for his horse and corn and fodder at the church to feed the horse, all the sample of the noble hospitality of those days, which was set by a noble good old brother of those days, Levi Truitt by name. Posey's name is famous throughout Western N. C., as one of the first pioneers in the Lord's kingdom here.

In 1842, Posey, as before stated moved to Georgia, and was present at the organization of the Georgia Baptist Convention.

Though he only lived about four years in his last adopted state, he endeared himself to them with whom he met and filled a very useful career there. Such was the esteem of the life and labors of Posey that a good Georgia brother wrote and published his life in book form. But with all the good and useful qualities of Posey, he like others had to die and pass away, and so on the 28th of December, 1846, he died beloved and full of good works in his 66th year and in the ministry forty years, having taken part in the organization of the Baptists of Western N. C. in the French Broad Association, 1807, remaining here long to see them planted in all these western counties, and also aiding in the State organization of Baptists in Ga.

Truly Posey labored and sowed and thousands of Christians have entered into his labors, many of whom have gone the way of all the earth, and many others, with hoary locks, are now, by reason of age, standing near the eternal home of the blessed, waiting the summons to go home.

Elder David Elder.

David Elder, the son of William Elder, was born about 1790. He was raised a poor boy and obtained his living by farming. He procured such an education as fitted him to read, write, etc.

He was married to Susan Hyde. a good woman to help in the race of life.

By this marriage there were five sons and six daughters. Three of the sons, William, Benjamin and John becoming Baptist preachers, the latter named becoming one of the most noted preachers in Texas where his father, David, finally settled about 1851.

Where David Elder joined the church at first, we cannot say, but we find his name in the organization of Brush church as a Deacon as early as Dec. 1832. His impressions lead him into the ministry and he was ordained to that work in Brush Creek July meeting 1834, by Elders Humphrey Posey, Joshua Hall; Joshua Ammons and a brother Styles.

From this time forth Elder was very active in Brush Creek, Lufty and Tennessee River churches He served Lufty church from its organization, 1836 to1842 in succession. He, in company with Elder James Kimsey aided in constituting Tennessee River in 1835.

Bro. Elder aided in ordaining Elder Samuel Gibson in Mt. Zion church on Lufty soon after his own ordination So we may consider Elder the first ordained preacher in the bounds of Tennessee River Association and Elder Gibson the second one.

Elder's timidity was very great at first. As an instance of such we give an incident of it. His first effort toward public life was to write out a prayer to be used by himself. This experiment did not fit him after putting it to a prayerful test and so one day, while in the silent woods where he had been at his devotions, he made a grave among the leaves and buried his written prayer to be used no more. In 1846 and 1847, brother Elder was the instrument under the Lord Jesus, aided by Elder Allen Ammons, who was then a Licentiate in conducting a precious revival of religion which extended its influence all over what is now Swain county, he, at the time, residing in about one mile of the present church of Cold Spring.

Brother Elder, like many other North Carolinians have done, in 1877 moved to Texas with most of his family, where he soon became missionary and preached until his death, about the year 1854. He was a sound gospel preacher, giving his churches and people good doctrine. He was also a good friend of education and missions.

Elder Samuel Gibson.

Samuel Gibson was born in Burke county, N. C., on the 15th day of August, 1794. He was the second son of Joseph and Gemima Gibson.

In his youthful days he had serious impressions in regard to the importance of the soul and the christian religion, which impressions kept him from joining some of the youthful follies of his day, such as dancing, cock-fighting, swearing, etc.

He was noted for his truthfulness and honesty. There was nothing hidden in his character, as he always spoke his sentiments and belief without any deceit or intention to be misunderstood

He enlisted in the service of his country in the war with Britain on the 9th of Deeember, 1813, and served faithfully until his discharge May 22nd, 1818.

He loved the union and throughout the war between the states he claimed and expressed his feelings and love for the "Stars and Stripes," notwithstanding his decendants were all fighting under the "Stars and Bars."

He was married to Eliza Jane Black in Burke county in February, 1818, in whom he found a perfect help-mate until in April, 1866, when death removed her to a better home.

He was subsequently married to Charity White, a good Christian woman, who gave him much comfort in his last days and who died soon after her husband. We turn to notice his early piety and his conversion to Christianity.

He professed faith in the blood of Jesus in the year 1830, and joined the Mt. Zion Baptist church, a church on the Oconee Lufty river, and which then belonged to the French Broad Association, and was baptized in said river, by Elder Adam Corn.

Elder Gibson was ordained to the Gospel ministry in the Mt. Zion Baptist church, in what is now Swain county, by Elders William Haynes and David Elder, as Presbytery, in the year 1834.

He was a zealous and faithful minister to tha time of his death which occurred in Macon county, N. C., on the 16th day of June, 1878.

The subject of this memoir was a strong advocate of the cause of Temperance, and if an extremist on any one point it was that of Temperance.

Elder Gibson's education was limited though being, perhaps over the ordinary scholarship of his day. He served as magistrate in the county of Haywood for many years, was punctual to his business engagements.

He would never disappoint a congregation or a church, but always met his appointments. The days of this venerable servant of God were spent financially in the counties of N. C. west of the Balsam mountains where his footprints were often made and his voice of gospel-teaching was heard for more than forty years. His heart and soul abounded in the principles of charity, and although not what the world calls wealthy, he lived free from want and was liberal to the needy.

His rule of domestic life was to follow the pursuits of husbandry, or tillage of the earth about four days in each week and attend his ministerial engagements the other three. He delighted to labor with his hands and did so until afflicted beyond ability to do so.

His ministry was spent mostly in Haywood, Macon, Cherokee, Jackson and Swain counties. he dwelling in what is now Swain for about twenty years. His membership was in Cowee Baptist church from 1851 or 1852 until his death.

His zeal for piety and the good cause of Truth did not abate with the advancement of age, but with a spirit somewhat akin to the Leaders of ancient Isreal, viz: Moses, Joshua, David and Solomon he desired to deliver his farewell warnings and councils to the churi es. From 1866 to 1876, he traveled around among the churcl which had been the scenes of his youthful labors and preached, as termed them, his farewell sermons. Heat of summer and cold winter and the high mountains of Cowee and their neighbori ranges were traversed to make these farewell pilgrimages to the d churches he loved so well. He believed that the call to the Minis was the impressions of God's Holy Spirit upon the man, feeling it be his duty to preach and teach men to repent and live Godly lives this present world in order to gain that which is to come throu the atoning merits of Jesus Christ.

Elder James Kimzey.

Rev. James Kimzey, late Moderator of the Valley River Baptist Association, died on Tuesday evening, April 12th, 1870, at his own house, in Towns county, Georgia, in the sixty-seventh year of his age, and in the midst of his usefulness as a minister of the Gospel.

Elder Kimzey was, perhaps, the most successful preacher in all the mountain country of North Carolina and Georgia. He was one of the few that continued at his post throughout the late war in the States. He was the son of Thomas and Nancy Kimzey. Was born in Haywood county, N. C., December 23rd, 1803. He joined the Baptist church in Franklin, was baptized in the Tennessee river by Rev. H. Posey, September 6th, 1830, and commenced preaching shortly after as a licentiate in that church. Was ordained afterwards by Elders H. Posey, J. Hall, G. F. Caler and B. Stiles. He continued a faithful, zealous, and much respected minister of the Gospel for near forty years. The circumstances of his dying bed are so remarkable that a slight sketch will be noticed here.

On Monday, the 11th of April, his condition showed plainly to the bystanders that he could not last long. This being suggested to him by a friend, he summoned all his remaining strength, and in the full possession of all the faculties of his mind, commenced exhorting the crowd of bystanders around his dying bed; and with but momentary intervals, continued his exhorting until Tuesday in the afternoon, when his breathing stopped, and he sank down in death without a sigh or a groan, remarking that *his work was done.*

Well might Balaam say: "Let me die the death of the righteous, and let my last end be like his." Num. 23:10. Elder Kimzey's funeral was conducted by Elders E. Hedden and A. Corn. Hedden opened the services, and read for his text Heb. 11:4. "He being dead yet speaketh." A. Corn followed on the same words. And the services closed by saying "our brother has gone to rest, and his works will follow him." Rev. 14.

The good works of brother Kimzey may never be fully known in this life. "He often went forth weeping, but would return rejoicing, bringing his sheaves with him." Pas. 12:6. He traveled and preached much as a missionary, mostly on his own expense; and all the while having the pastoral care ot one or more churches, which he attended monthly with great exactness. His pulpits were seldom left empty on preaching days. He was married to the daughter of Matthew and Resine Russell, of the Presbyterian order, consequently their daughter would be raised under the rules and discipline of that church, which eminently fitted her for the duties of subsequent life. She was born in Pickens district, S. C., in the year 1804, was married to James Kinzey in 1824—were both baptized in Tennessee river, by Rev. H. Posey, and received into the Baptist church in Franklin. There seems to have been a blessing concealed in this marriage not then perceivable, but was afterwards fully developed in their qualifications for usetulness in future life—he as a minister of Jesus, and she as a suitable and faithful companion and help meet in all his gloomy forebodings incident to ministerial life. Like an angel of peace, she was always ready to administer to his necessities, and to keep the bright side always turned towards him.

In many of his missionary travels she accompanied him, sometimes for weeks, or even months, at a time. Over mountains, and across rivers, her face, like an angel of light, was there to cheer and encourage him in the duties of his calling as a minister of Jesus. And if he traveled alone, which he often did, she was always ready at the door on his return with a hearty "How have you done?" But after toiling in this way, for near forty years, sometimes happy, but often cast down, afflicted and distressed, this angel of peace sickened and died! She filled her day—she did it well! and is now, we trust, wearing that triumphant crown that is prepared for all the faithful in Christ Jesus. The spot where her body lies is holy ground, sacred, precious, and will keep sacred the blest deposit until Christ shall bid it rise.

But the surviuing partner is left alone to meet and buffet the storms of life, with no bosom friend to tell his sorrows to—none but Jesus, the friend, of sinners; to tell his troubles to! But still he faltered not. His preaching seemed, if possible, to possess more power and influence as he grew older. Revivals sprang up in nearly all the churches and settlements where he preached—many joined the churches under his care. and were baptized by him. We might name some of them. The brother Hills—Noah and Wade—and brother Heddens—Elisha and Jefferson—names that adorn the pages of our history as much as any others, were raised up under his preaching, and were baptized by him.

He was not what the world calls rich nor learned, but having a competency, he was like one we read of. "Mighty in the Scriptures." Acts 18:24. He never took notes, nor wrote even the skeleton of a sermon. All his discourses were delivered with feeling and force of argument, as well as Scripture—almost irresistable! And when he indulged in exhortation, which he often did, he had no superior. His words were delivered with a force of feeling that must be felt by all his hearers. He was generous to a fault. He wrs affable and kind in his intercourse with mankind generally, and in return was beloved by all. He was a kind and indulgent parent, and a loving companion. He left nine children living, four boys and five girls.

He was twice married. His second wife was a Baptist by profession, and the widow of Samuel Cathey, Esq., of Towns county, Georgia. But he is gone!—has left a disconsolate widow and many friends, to mourn his unexpected departnre. He has finished his work, as said in his last words. "*My work is done!*" His breathing stopped, and he sank down in death without a sigh or groan, and now, we trust, beyond the reach of trouble!—has joined that dear departed companion of his, who had reached those blissful regions but a few years before.

JAMES WHITAKER, SR.

James Whitaker, Sr.

James Whitaker, Sen., was the son of Joshua and Mary Whitaker, was born April 3, 1779, in Rowan county, N. C., near the place where Lexington now stands, (now Davidson county) and was the younges of four brothers and two sisters, of poor parents, and was a Farme by occupation. His chance for an education was very limited, neve having gone to school after his tenth year. His parents were of the High Church party, and according to their rules had him sprinkled when he was quite young; but this, according to his own statement had but little weight on his mind. In September 1800, Bro. Whitaker married Polly Walker, daughter of Howard Walker, and shortly after moved to Buncombe county, N. C., then a newly settled county. Bro. Whitaker joined the Church on French Broad, May the 3rd or 5th, 1806, and on the 10th of the same Month became a consistent member of the Cane Creek Church, and was ordained Deacon, and elected Clerk and Treasurer at the same time. Bro. Whitaker, has been Clerk and Deacon in all the Churches to which he has ever belonged, and has clerked for all the Associations where his lot has been cast. A great portion of his life has been spent in serving the public, both in Church and State, he wrote a great deal, both secular and religious, both for the press and otherwise. Bro. Whitaker, having lost his first wife, when quite old, married Mary McBrayer, widow of James McBrayer, a highly respectable old lady, and a member of the Baptist Church, with whom he spent his remaining days on earth in comparative tranquility. Something over four years before his death he got a fall, from the effects of which he never recovered, having to walk on crutches the balance of his days, during which time he did tle else than talk, read and write, the latter of which he did a great al of, and his writings are now on file in his desk. Bro. Whitaker is spent a long life of usefulness, both to Church and State, and in s death the Church has lost one of her main props, as he was a faithl and consistent Baptist to the day of his death. Bro. Whitaker ad a good head, and a wonderfully strong mind, which he retained to great extent to the last, and his general health was good; but, on onday before his death, his strength failed him so that he required ssistance, and for the four days that he lived he suffered a great deal; ut he had some happy seasons, he slept about half his time; but hen not asleep nor suffering too much, he was talking words of encouragement to Christians, warning sinners, and pronouncing blessings on all his friends. A few hours before his death he told the writer f these lines that he was passing from life to death, and from death life again. He clasped his hands and shouted. "Glory! Glory!! lory!!!" He then said he saw his happy home in Heaven, and ried to describe it. On being asked if he was happy, he exclaimed, O, yes, happy, happy!" He said he saw that beautiful crown of ever-fading glory prepared for him, the beauties of which he said he ould not describe and at 50 minutes past 4 o'clock on Thursday eveing, the fourth day of his confinement, he calmly passed away; but e believe that our loss is his eternal gain. In view of these things, et us all try to be prepared to meet our Father and brethren in a etter land than this.

JAMES WHITAKER, Jun.

Elder John L. Crisp.

We having been appointed by the church of Stecoah, now attempt to write a brief biographical sketch of the Rev. John L. Crisp. "The pulpit is the most favorable arena for the cultivation and display of eloquence which the usages and institutions of modern times present." The inherent dignity and importance of the subjects which he is called upon to discuss; the responsibility he is under for the truth or falsehood of the doctrines which he inculcates, the immense influence exerted by christianity upon the laws, literature and social economy of the community; the long array of impressive historical associations, which are connected with the past fortunes and vicissitudes of the most ancient, and potent of all existing institutions; the fact that the preacher is supposed to be a man of spotless character; all these reasons and many more that might be enumerated, often render the pulpit the throne of eloquence. But it is a fact to be lamented, that the preachers of our mountain country are generally without much education. and have to labor under very limited circumstances. The subject of our present memoir was a man of noted piety, of firm Baptist principles earnestly contending for the faith once for all delivered to the saints. Brother Crisp, the son of Micager and Mary Crisp was born May the 25th A. D. 1818, in Burke county, now Caldwell, was married to Percy Hogue in 1837. On Sept. the 8th, A. D. 1843, he was received by baptism into the fellowship of the Valley River Church, the ordinance being administered by the Rev. James Kimsey, and in the year 1844 was dismissed by letter and became a member o. the Stecoah Church, now Tennessee River, at the time of its constitution and remained a member of that church until the constitution of the

New Prospect church now Stecoah. Bro. John L. Crisp was ordained to the work of the ministry, September the 27th, A. D. 1873, by Rev. Allen Ammons and M. Ghormley, Bro. Crisp remained a member of the Stecoah Church up to the time of his death. He departed this life May the first A. D. 1876, age 57 years 11 months and 6 days. The cause of his death is supposed to have been Paralysis. He survived only about 11 hours after he was stricken, being speechless most of the time, communicating to the satisfaction of all, by signs that he was going to change this time world for an heavenly. During the meeting protracted from the sermon in his memory there were over fifty accessions to the church. He was a devoted and faithful member and did much to advance the Master's kingdom. He was always ready to lend a helping hand to the indigent and helpless. His obliging and benevolent disposition gained for him the good will of all who knew him. It may be said that he lived an exemplary life. We feel sad to think he will no more meet with us in laying plans to advance the Redeemer's kingdom and to win souls for Christ; nevertheless we kindly submit to the will of our King and Great High Priest, the Lord Jesus Christ. When the family draw their chairs around the fireside. during the chilly winds of autumn, which sigh through the trees, they behold a vacant seat never more to be filled; the loved and cherished one who has "passed over the river" and now resting under the trees of life in the land of sweet deliverance. "There remaineth therefore a rest for the people of God." We extend to the bereft wife, sons and daughters our heart felt sympathies, and hope they will fight the good fight, and run with patience the race that is set before them so that they may be able to meet the departed one beyond the skies.

T. A. Carpenter; Joel L. Crisp.

Elder Allen Ammons.

Eld. Allen Ammons was born in Buncombe County, N. C.. Sept. 1819. He emigrated with his parents, Ephraim and Nancy Ammons, to Macon Co., N. C. His parents being among the first to settle this county, was not able to give him the advantage of an early education, no regular schools being established, so that the high character that he acquired as a preacher was due under God, to his deep piety, sound sense and unceasing efforts to educate himself in the work to which he was called.

He professed faith in Christ in his 17th year and was baptized by Elder Humphrey Posey into the fellowship of Franklin Baptist church. He was married Feb. 22nd, 1840, to Miss Cyntha, daughter of Manuel and Margaret Ross. Eld. Ammons lived in different localities of this county for some three or four years. In his 24th year he furnished strong evidence of his Divine call to the work of the Ministry and preached his first sermon in Bro. Bennet Crisp's house, some of the oldest brethren and sisters of this (Stecoah) vicinity remember his first sermon. He "conferred not with flesh and blood," but consulted only, the Master of the Vineyard and at his bidding he went. He identified himself with Brush Creek Baptist church, Macon Co., N. C., and his membership remained with said church till the Master called him from his work.

Elder Ammons was ordained, June 3rd, 1848, to the full work of the ministry by Elders S. Gibson and S. Jabcob Mingus, and from that time till now his name has been a household word among the Baptists of this entire section of country. As a preacher, Elder Ammons had but few equals. He was always sound in doctrine, and his rmons were especially noticeable for their deep solemnity and the arnestness with which they were delivered. The hearts of his hears were moved by his tender and earnest persuasions, while their minds were enlightened by his clear logic. There are hundreds of men and women throughout this country who can remember a great part of many of his sermons, his style was so impressive. While he as a man of strong will and of remarkable firmness, when he came to talk for his Master, it was with eyes overflowing and with words of impassionate tenderness. As a preacher, his loss is greatly felt in this, the Tennessee River Association. For several successive years e saw him fill the Moderators chair in this Association. As a man nd a citizen, he was upright in his conduct, and his religion was his uide. As a christian, he possessed strong faith, and in fact, his enre life and teachings go to furnish conclusive proof of his true and enuine christianity. As a husband and father, none can ever know is worth save the bereft widow and children, whoso hearts are made esolate by his death.

He kept no record of the number he baptized (as we can find) but e are satisfied he baptized more than one thousand persons during is ministry. He was engaged in the Masters work about thirty-two ears. He labored as pastor and missionary and ever seemed to submit himself to the demand and call of the Master. He left the comorts of home and became Captain of the 30th N. C. Regiment, subjecting himself to the hardships of camp and soldier life for about hree years. He was an industrious minded man and while preaching thirty-two years, nearly at his own expenses, managed to secure a espectable legacy for his wife and children. His death was very sudden, his suffering great, though he was in his proper mind and manifested great patience, and met the summons with perfect submission. When asked by his son, if he would have a Doctor sent for, he calmly eplied, the Lord is my Doctor, and in a few minutes his body slept and his soul had gone to God who gave it.

He was stricken with Paralysis at his residence in Swain Co., N. C., uly 2nd, 1880, and died in about three hours after he received the troke. His remains lie in the tomb within less than one fourth of a nile of his residenee, to await the call on the resurrection morn.

W. D. Crisp, Chm'n.

Elder Wesley Williams.

Wesley Williams, when a little helpless infant, was found at the well of a man by the name of Williams in Pickens district, South Carolina, in the year 1835. Mr. Williams, Pharaoh's daughter-like, took the subject of our sketch and raised him as his own son, and it was from his adopted parent that Wesley Williams received his name. Elder Williams never had the satisfaction of knowing any blood relation.

He was given a limited common School education. Like many of his age and time, he was a soldier in the war of Secession in which he received injuries which never healed sufficiently to permit him to ride on horseback. He was in the noted "Blow Up" at Petersburg, Va., if we mistake not, which was the closing scene of his military life.

We have no account of Elder Williams' religious life prior to his being licensed to preach the gospel, which was done by Concord Baptist church, Henry county, Alabama, Jan. 16th, 1864, only a short time after he joined the church. He was ordained to the ministry by a presbytery consisting of Solomon Hargrove, Samuel J. Knowles and Moses Bracken, July 19th, 1864.

From the time of his entry into the Christian ministry, Brother Williams led one of the most consecrated and active lives for his Master, Christ.

Having entered upon the Christian warfare, he determined to equip himself well with its weapon of defense, by studying the Holy Scriptures, and as a consequence, his reading excelled anything we have any account of. We think he claimed to have read the Old Testament through thirty times and the New Testament three hundred times during his life.

Extensive were his missionary labors, and we are surprised, almost, at his abounding activity in this sphere of work, when we consider that it was all done on foot. He labored under the appointment of the Home Mission Board of the Southern Baptist Convention, travelling and preaching in all the counties in the State of Florida.

Elder Williams' activity and success are proven by the results of his work as he aided in organizing about two hundred churches and baptized seven hundred and seventy-nine persons during his ministry.

On a missionary tour, he arrived in Swain county, N. C., February 1874, in the tenth year of his ministry. So exhilarating was the mountain climate of Western North Carolina, in contrast with what our brother had endured in Florida, that he finally concluded to locate here, and so he united with Forney's Creek church, of Tennessee River Baptist Association, by a letter from a church of West Florida Baptist Association, in April 1874.

Not willing to be alone, our subject sought for a helpmate, which he soon found in the person of Miss Salinda Jane Crawford, to whom he was united in matrimony, April 30th, 1874, and settled as a citizen of Swain county, N. C., in the neighborhood of Forney's Creek, where he lived until he ended his life work.

Here, in his new field of labor, he was chosen Association Missionary at the session of the Association in 1874 and again in 1875, in which place he labored acceptably until his death, March 25th, 1876. He also filled the place of pastor in Forney's Creek, Cold Spring, and Tennessee River churches, during his brief career here. The last sermon he preached was at Forney's Creek church, Saturday, March 11th, 1876.

On the 14th of March '76, he was taken very sick with a fever and after severe suffering for 11 days, which he endured with Christian patience, he fell asleep, March 25th, 1874. Thus ended the life of this beloved servant of God, at the age of forty-one years, and in the thirteenth year of his Christian pilgrimage.

His winning disposition and pious zeal made him popular and respected, and his loss to the church, Association and citizenship was mourned by many. Elder Williams was about 5 ft. 7 in. high, slightly gray eyes and rather dark flaxen hair, his weight being about 140 or 150 pounds.

He was interred in the graveyard in sight of Tuckaseige river about one and one half miles below the mouth of Forney's Creek.

Elder Joshua Potts Edwards.

Elder J. P. Edwards was born March, 1st. 1818, in Washington county. Tennessee

In the 23rd year of his age, he made a profession of religion, uniteing with Greasy Cove Baptist church in the same county of his birth, and was baptized by Elder Baily. Soon after his baptism, he was licensed to preach after which his time was principally spent in preaching and teaching.

Elder Edwards was married twice. His first wife was a Miss Arenith Matcher with whom he lived four years when she died. His second marriage was to Miss Elizabeth Massay, March 16th. 1849.

In 1848, he moved to Cherokee county N. C., and joined the Friendship Baptist church, and still later he joined Beech Creek church.

In 1866, he moved to Beech Creek, (now Graham county,) and became a member of Cheoah Baptist church, and later on his membership was with Tuskeega and Stecoah churches. He was ordained to the ministry in Tuskeega church in 1878.

He filled the pastorates of Tuskeega, Stecoah, Tennessee River and Hazel Creek churches for a number of years. He was a Bible student, zealous in his labors and sound in doctrine.

He took great delight in talking on religious subjects, and whatever the topic of conversation, it would find some channel through which to flow to Jesus. He read much and retained much of what he read.

When too feeble to fill his appointments he spent his time at home with his family.

He suffered for two years with Cancer of the stomach, but bore his sufferings patiently, often saying that Jesus suffered for him and he was willing to suffer until Jesus called him home.

He fell asleep July 30th, 1885, as quietly as a babe upon its mother's bosom.

After the shadow of death had commenced its final work upon the vitals of his mortal life, he said all was well and that he would soon be relieved from pain. Even after he had so far passed that he could not speak, he was asked by his son if his way was clear, and he pointed up and noded his head.

Thus ended his life work at the age of sixty-seven years, four months and twenty-nine days

W. D. Crisp.

Elder Isaac Taylor Sims Sherrill.

Elder I. T. S. Sherrill, son of ——— and ——— Sherrill was born in Coffee county, Tennessee, about 1812. He was given a liberal English education. At about the age of 18 or 20 years, he had become a professor of religion and connected himself to the Methodists where he soon became what is termed an itinerent minister, in which connection he labored for seven years. But his investigation of the subject of Christian duty finally led him to abandon the Methodists and join the Baptists. He was baptized by the noted Elder Howell, of Nashville, Tenn.

Our subject was soon ordained to the Baptist ministry and continued preaching.

In 18— he came to North Carolina. He was married to Caroline Sherrill, daughter of that worthy veteran, Samuel Sherrill about 1854. From this time forth, his labors as a minister was spent principally in the counties of Jackson, Macon, Cherokee and Swain, N. C.

His membership was at Shoal Creek Baptist church for several years and subsequently at Cold Spring and Indian Creek churches. Elder Sherrill's pastorate with Cold Spring commenced about the year 1855.

He served New Prospect or Stecoah church, we think for a while. He was a strong Baptist and well read in church history and his public career covered a period of over fortyfive years. Elder Sherrill was o a lively and pleasant social disposition, though for several years his sermons often abounded with strong utterances against Methodism and other sects by which he often received the epithet of "Fight-r." He was eloquent and when warmed with his subject, he had ew equals in the pulpit.

As he grew older, his preaching was less filled with invectives against he denominations.

While he may be styled a good preacher, he was not so excellent in discipline as some.

One of the greatest strokes of his life, was the apparent coolness of some of his ministering brethren toward him which grew out of reports against his ministerial and Christian character, leading to an nvestigation of the charges by Cold Spring, his church, but from which he came forth with an honorable acquittal.

His views on the subject of temperance with the floaitng rumors against him, greatly injured his reputation, but with all his trials he had to encounter, he was a good man who loved his Master's cause. He lost his dear wife in 187— which seemed to confuse him for a ime. He formed a second marriage to Catherine Green, a widow. He raised three sons and two daughters by his first wife. He was afflicted with a severe pain in his thumb which resulted in his death ———— 1886. His last words to surviving friends were full of hope as he gave testimony of a happy acceptance with Christ Jesus.

James M. Thomasson.

James M. Thomasson, son of Lemuel Thomasson. was born in York District. S. C.. May 18, 1809.

His parents were wealthy and owned slaves. His education was equal to the best advantages given in the country schools of his day and time, being sufficient to read, write and to calculate in first principles of Arithmetic.

He came to Macon connty, N. C., when a young man and was engaged for a time in the mercantile pursuit.

He was also a teacher of schools, both common and musical, and his labors in these were very acceptable as he took great pains to start the young learner.

As it was custom in earlier days, he prepared his note books, containing about thirteen tunes, such as Olney, Holy Mana, New Britain, Midnight Cry, etc., in manuscript both notes and words, printing them with his pen, for each one of his singing classes.

In his common school work, he was very diligent, and some of his pupils have never forgotten his efforts to start them in their school studies.

Brother Thomasson was married to Susan Truitt daughter of Levi and ——— Truitt, Dec. 9th, 1832, by whom he raised three sons and seven danghters who were brought up on the farm on Brush Creek in one mile of Brush Creek Baptist church. Our subject was converted and joined Brush Creek church 18— and was baptized by Elder Humphrey Posey. He was soon elected church clerk, which place he effisiently filled first and last for over thirty years. He was chosen deacon of Brush Creek church, to which he was ordained in onnection with Solomon Truitt, by Jacob Mingus and Samuel Gibon at June meeting 1848.

Our subject was a staunch Baptist and always set a good example n church attendauce and church councils and supporting the gospel. He loved the church and was true to it and his heavenly Master.

He served Tennessee River Association in the clerkship during the years 1874 and 1876.

He was a man of disease for several years which combined with the nfirmities of age kept him from attending church for a few years prior to his death, but with all these he was patient to the last when he calmly fell asleep in Jesus, March 16th, 1891, at the age of 81 years,) months and 28 days

Elder Jesse Madison Smiley.

Elder J. M. Smiley, son of Jesse and Elizabeth L. Smiley, was born in Rutherford county, N. C., Nov. 19th, 1820, being the second of three sons and ten daughters and third child of the family.

His father, Jesse Smiley, was raised an orphan boy, whose parents died when he was only old enough to recollect the death, in consequence of which he was bound to a man by the name of Smith. By this the exact time of his birth was lost, but he was born in Dinwidie county, Va., about the year 1781. Smith was a hard, unfeeling master who treated the orphan boy like a negro by whom he received no schooling and as a result Jesse Smiley was an unlettered man.

He lived with Smith until 15 years of age when he left him to shift for himself.

He married twice, his first wife dying without children. His second wife, Elizabeth Harrison, was born in Brunswick county, Va., June 8th, 1796, and she was the pious Baptist and devoted Christian mother of him who heads this sketch. Jesse Smiley, the father, was also a Baptist, and although not taught in letters, he had a vivid memory, sound judgment and industrious habits, obtaining his living by farming.

He was a poor man, but he owned a home, kept his family free from want, and gave all his children that lived to be grown, an education sufficient to read, write, and some of them obtained to a knowledge of Arithmetic and Grammar.

Such as the foregoing, was the parentage of Elder J. M. Smiley, whose life and labors we now wish to narate. He attended the schools of the old log school house three months and seventeen days in the ubscription schools of the time which was all the schooling he ever eceived, but by his aptness and attention to his studies he learned to ead, write and calculate through the four rules of Arithmetic.

He followed the occupation of farming as the principal one, but he was also a mechanic and could perform several kinds of mechanism.

He was united in holy matrimony to Annie Brendle, daughter of John D. and Lottie Brendle, Dec. 3rd, 1842.

His wife, Annie, was born July 13th, 1827, and had been given but little schooling, barely enough to read print; but she loved the help of good books and was a devoted wife and mother, just such as a poor minister needs to see over his household. The result of this wedding was six sons and seven daughters.

Elder Smiley was converted in his fourteenth year during a protracted spell of sickness, but he did not make a public profession there. nor did he profess until after a severe stroke of sickness in his family, in July 1855, when the good Lord called away two of his children by death. This sad affliction set him to seeking for the evidence of his salvation which took place under the ministry of Elder Merritt Rickman in October, 1855.

He joined the Baptist church at Cold Spring in March, 1856, and was baptized by Elder Samuel Gibson in Alarka on the farm of Nathan DeHart. He was soon chosen Clerk of Cold Spring church, in which he labored for about seven years. He put off what he often felt to be his duty, that of preaching, for the long years, before he made his first effort, which effort was made in the house of his father-in-law on one Sunday evening in Dec., 1866. His first text was "Wherefore He saith, Awake thou that sleepest and arise from the dead and Christ shall give thee light," Eph. 5:14.

He was ordained to the gospel ministry in Cold Spring Baptist church in July 1871, by Elders M. Rickman, A. A. Justice, W. H. Conner and P. R. Rickman.

Elder Smiley labored in the ministry about seven years before he was ordained.

His life work in the cause of Christ has been confined principally to Swain county, N. C., where he has labored at a great sacrifice of his time as pastor in Cold Spring, Holly Spring, Forney's Creek, Indian Creek, Tennessee River and perhaps some other churches, and as Missionary of the Tennessee River Association from Autumn of 1881 to 1882, one year. Elder Smiley's rule was to visit the destitute and preach, and in this way he was instrumental under God in preparing a people for building Forney's Creek and Indian Creek churches. He held protracted meetings in several other places and in all has assisted in organizing ten churches, all in the bounds of Tennessee River Association, and four ministers and several deacons.

He has baptized many, and many more have been converted under his preaching.

Elder Smiley has been a close Bible student and few excelled him in a knowledge of the Bible. Most of his preaching has been done at his own charges; in fact he often refused remuneration in his early ministry, to his hurt, we think.

His health and strength have been such that he would do much manuel labor and fill his preaching appointments, but in 1889, his health failed in consequence of a lung trouble, and he had to slacken his public service.

He was able to attend the Association at his home church, Cold Spring, in August 1890, and to make a Sunday school speech in the Sunday school mass-meeting on Sunday morning from which we drew much of his childhood impressions and early conversion. He visited Indian Creek church and preached on the 1st Sunday in Oct., 1890, which was his last preaching service.

His disease, Consumption, continued its dreadful ravages, which our subject bore with Christian patience, remarking that it was going to take him away and that it would be the better for him, and at 12,50 p. m. Sunday, July 12th, 1891, he quietly fell asleep and passed into the spirit world at the age of 70 years, 7 months and 20 days.

Elder A. A. Justice.

Amos A. Justice, son of James D. and Anthrite Justice, was born in Henderson county, N. C., two miles south of Hendersonville, in sight of old Mud Creek Baptist church, Feb. 9th, 1823, in which period Amos learned little else than wickedness.

He was brought up to the occupation of the farm and enjoyed the pleasures of country life.

In 1831, his father married a second time and collected the children home. It was fortunate for the orphans that their step mother was, to use the words of the subject of this sketch, "One of the best women in the world," by whose help the children received due care. These parents were not religious but they instructed the children in good morals, and to respect religious people.

The mother of Elder Justice had left her dying request and prayer that her children prepare to meet her in heaven. This was the prayer of her who had lived and died a consistent Christian of the Baptist church.

The request of his dead mother was told to Elder Justice, when he had arrived to riper years, by his father, and the words of the request rang in his ears and reached his heart. He then and there vowed to forsake sin, but rude company led him astray again. After spending Sunday, April 30th, 1838, in desecration instead of going to preaching and Sunday school, Monday morning May 1st opened upon him with sad reflections over his misspent Sunday when his mother's last words again spoke to his heart, resulting in a renewal of the vow to forsake sin, followed by a prayer. His conviction of sin burdened him sorely and he tried the law for pardon which failed and with the aid of God and the instructions of his brother, T. B. Justice, he was led to the end of his own strength, and gave up all worldly hope on the 1st Sunday night in July, 1838, and found pardon by fully trusting Christ. With the acceptance of sins pardoned, he sawa t once, a fullness in Jesus to save all that would come to him by true repentance and faith, and felt it his duty to persuade others to come to Christ.

Being only a youth of fifteen years of age at his conversion, he would not join the church without his father's permission, and at the expiration of one month in obedience to his father's advice to wait thus, he joined Ebenezer Baptist church, four miles east of Hendersonville, N. C., 4th Sunday in August, 1838, followed by his father who also joined on the same day, and he, our subject. was baptized by Elder Benjamin King.

His educational advantages were limited, but he was given schooling, in the old-time log school house, sufficiently to read, write and calculate in Arithmetic, to the Rule of Three.

Immediately following his baptism, he had the answer of a good conscience toward God, was very happy and had stronger impressions to exhort others to seek salvation.

His impressions and gifts were early discovered by the ministers, John Lyons, James Blythe, and R. Jordan, who advised him to make an effort, but fear and timidity kept him from doing so more than to offer public prayer, sometimes. In September, 1847, he moved to Macon county, where he subsequently married Margaret L. Shoap, daughter of Jacob and Isabella Shoap, of Burningtown.

He hoped that the impressions to preach would leave him but they did not.

In 1852, he engaged in the work of selling books and distributing tracts as a colporteur of the American Tract and Bible Society which business he followed with success until March, 1860, when he was compelled to stop this business on account of the death of his dear wife who had been one of the most faithful companions in the world. Thus our subject was left with three children and no good wife to longer guide his house, a stroke which he deeply realized for years.

He formed, after a time, a second marriage to Mary Simonds, in whom he found another worthy companion true to his interests.

By both marriages the Lord has given our brother five sons and three daughters.

He put off the duty of preaching until in 1862, when the church, Fort Lindsay, considered his gift and licensed him to preach, and at the expiration of three months, under the announcement of his pastor, William K. Adams, our brother made his first effort to preach which was from Isaaih 1:5,6. The Lord blessed the sermon which was followed by twenty-five persons asking prayers as seekers and twelve or fifteen professing faith in Christ.

On the solicitations of Brush Creek, Cold Spring and other churches, Elder Justice was set forward for ordination, by his home church, Fort Lindsay, and in November, 1862, he was solemnly ordained to the full functions of the gospel ministry by Elders Samuel Gibson and Allen Ammons as the presbytery.

Thus he was enstalled and entered upon a most useful career in the Lord's work as an under Shepherd as the little flocks at Cold Spring, Brush Creek, Stecoah, Liberty, Cartoogaghaye and many other places can testify. He has aided in organizing several churches and ordaining several deacons and ministers.

He has spent much of his time in visiting destitute sections and by such aided in preparing the way for church organization. He has generally had charge of from one to four churches as pastor which labors have generally been prosperous. He has twice filled the exalted station of Moderator of his Association, Tennessee River, and one year he filled the place of Association missionary. He is now 68 years old, but his love and zeal for his Master's work still prompts him onward in the good work, and it is hoped, though enfeebled by the weight of years, that many more years will be spared to him by his Lord to serve the church.

Life Sketch of Elizabeth Crisp.

Elizabeth Crisp, daughter of George Holloway, a Methodist minister, was born in Burke county, N. C., February, 15th. 1787, and is now living at the advanced age of 103 years.

She was raised up under Methodist influence, as we see, and became a member of that denomination in her fifteenth year, which is the beginning period of her religion's life.

She was married to Bennett Crisp in her twenty-fourth year, by whom she raised five sons and three daughters. Pendleton, John Bennett, George Crisp and Robert Crisp are her sons

Her posterity has increased, and now she enjoys the pleasure of having seen her children and children's children to the fifth generation.

Old as mother Crisp is, she has her proper mind and can talk with good judgement.

She could see to thread a sewing needle when more than 100 years old, and was enabled to sew.

But one of the most remarkable incidents of her life is, that she, after spending her long life in the Methodist church until April — 1891, when she joined the Tennessee River Baptist church and was baptized by Elder Robert Crisp, her grandson.

In her statement to the brethren and church, when she joined, she said she was not satisfied to die until baptized like her Lord. "I have done this," said she, "to please my Lord and myself."

Deacon John DeHart.

John DeHart, son of Nathan and Catherine DeHart, was born in Burke county, N. C., Nov. 26th, 1804.

His parents moved to Tennesseee about the time of his first recollection, where they dwelt a short time, and from there they moved and finally settled in Wayne Co., Kentucky, on a creek called, Johnson's Fork, where our subject was brought up to the occupation of farming.

Like so many of his day and generation, he was deprived of an education on account of the meagre chances afforded him in youth, and so he had to brave life's battles without book knowledge.

Truthful, honest, sober and industrious, he grew up among a family of several children, of whom he was the elder, and made a man of strong judgement, active effort, and determination.

He was married to Jane Roberts, a woman well fitted by her fine womanly qualities to make our subject a good wife, which marriage took place Oct. 18, 1823. His noble consort had some education and could read the Bible which was the guide of the couple in subsequent life.

In October, 1828, our subject, with his wife and two children, Lydia and Martin, moved to Macon county, N. C., and located the first year on the Hale farm opposite the mouth of Cowee. From this place, he moved to a farm on the west bank of Tennessee river, now the farm of his grandson, A. J. Freeman, a short distance from Brush Creek church, where he resided nine years on State's land.

While here, he became well acquainted with several of the noted Cherokee Indians, who were his neighbors, dwelling along the Nantahala river, as they had not yet been removed by the United States. Uchella, the Chief, Old Charlie and Sal were Mr. DeHart's nearest neighbors in those pioneer days, and to the honor of those simple children of these mountains, they respected their white neighbor's live stock, always furnishing him information as to its whereabouts and sometimes, as a neighborly act, would bring it home to the owner.

Few families of the whites dwelt in what is now Swain county at that early day, and it fell to the lot of our subject to aid in opening the first public road down Tennessee river about the year 1830.

It was the good fortune of our subject to listen to the preaching of Humphrey Posey, G. F. Caler and others at this early day, and it was Posey's and Caler's preaching that fastened conviction for sin on his mind; but not until the loss of a dear child by drowning in Tennessee river, did he fully see his deep depravity and need of salvation.

Thus convicted, he wrestled with the Lord and found peace to his soul, on his knees, on the bank of the river, in secret. He confessed Christ in baptism at the hands of Elder G. F. Caler, thus becoming a member of Brush Creek church, 1834. He was ordained a Deacon in Brush Creek 183—, and was in the organization of Cold Spring Baptist church in May, 1851.

Like most new converts, our subject was made to doubt his regeneration, at first, but the Savior gave him an answer of peace, after praying and inquiring about the matter in these words which seemed almost like a dream: "I will be with thee in the sixth trouble and will not forsake thee in the seventh:" this made him happy and strengthened his faith.

About the year 1838, he bought the Joe Sherrill place on Alarka, for $866.25, where he soon settled and prospered as a dutiful Christian and citizen. He was a member of the Board of Education and Warden of the Poor in Macon for seven or eight years.

Only three families resided above Brother DeHart on Alarka, at the time of his settlement here, viz: Ute Sherrill, Dock Wiggins and a Pendley. Here on Alarka, thirteen children, eight males and five females, including those born elsewhere, completed his large and industrious family.

In July 3rd, 1886, God took his kind helpmate home, and our Brother was left alone.

Again in Aug. 25th, 1887, he formed a second marriage to Jane Owen, a respectable widow lady of the Methodist persuasion, to whom is accorded the lot of consoling our Brother in his advanced years.

The life habits of our dear brother in Israel are such as are well worthy of notice here. He was blessed with several thousand dollars worth of property, which he has, as a true parent, equally disposed of among his children, save a little he still holds for himself and wife. so he intends no waste in lawsuits.

The writer has known him for forty years and can truthfully, and with pleasure say that Bro. John DeHart is and has been truly good to the poor, and very liberal to the support of the gospel and church of which he is a member.

He has refused a dollar a bushel for his corn offered by speculators and let his poor laborers have it at seventy-five cents per bushel.

His promises were sure to be fulfilled to the letter, and his overflowing honor in giving weights and measures in disposing of meat and grain of which, through a provident life of industry and economy by the blessing of God, he always had plenty of, is worthy of mention and imitation.

And his hospitality abounded, so that his home was the refreshing place for many of the saints and others of his fellowmen and women.

As our brother approached the latter part of his 88th year, he took a careful review of his past life and to use his own words, said. "I feel that I have wronged no one, and have done some good in the world." He said that he was resting on that hope he gained on Tennessee river so long ago, and it saved it is the mercy of God, and not for anything good that I have done.

He was heard say at the burial of one of his children that he had often prayed at that graveyard for the salvation of his children.

He, in Dec., 1892, a few days before his death, had his coffin made, believing that the time of his departure was near. He walked and could attend to business near the house on Friday 23rd of Dec., but at night was taken very ill and on Sunday night, Dec. 25th, 1892, he calmly fell asleep to await the sound of Gabriel's trump, beloved and mourned.

Elder Merritt Rickman.

Merritt Rickman was born in Buncombe county, N. C., east of Fair View, August 6, 1812. He was married to Miss Sarah Sitton, Jan. 29, 1828, in his sixteenth year.

He had not the advantage of schools and to his beloved wife was accorded the honor of teaching him to read. He made advancement in his studies and prepared himself thus for his life work and became what is termed a "Self-made man," of whom his country and wife may justly be proud and thankful.

He was converted and joined the Baptist church at Cane Creek and was baptized by Elder Robert Jordan in the county of his birth.

He was subsequently licensed to preach by Mills River Baptist church, Sept. 24, 1836, in which he was ordained Aug. 27, 1837, by Elders Robert Jordan, David Blythe, James Blythe, Jacob Cantrell and Matthew Capps.

For about eighteen years Elder Rickman filled a prominent place in churches included in French Broad or Salem Baptist Associations. He preached some in Rutherford county and once attended the Baptist State Convention of N. C. at Raleigh, as a delegate. About the year 1854, he disposed of his property in Henderson county, N. C., purchased a splendid farm on Cowee creek in Macon county, where he soon became one of Macon's model citizens and one of Tuckaseige Association's leading ministers, for a period of about twenty years. Here, in his latter field of life and labors, his church membership was in Cowee Baptist church, where he was pastor about all the time during his residence in Macon. He was pastor of Burningtown, Franklin, Coweta, Savanah and perhaps others in Macon and Jackson, and of Brush Creek andCold spring in what is now Swain county. He once went and attended a church in Haywood county.

His influence and power for good was felt all over these western counties. Such was his zeal, activity and success that he became Moderator and Missionary in Tuckaseige Association, which he filled with great efficiency to the honor of his high calling and that of his denomination.

His home influence and example with his family were excellent, and his industry in manual labor on his farm was, we know, a good model for his church and people. He raised a large family of children of whom two sons, Josiah and Riley became ministers. He had plenty of this world's goods, and taught by precept and example, his people "To provide things honest in the sight of all men."

Elder Rickman, by his natural gifts which he cultivated and by which he acquired great ability in public speaking, made him unusually entertaining to his audiences.

His bright face, flashing eye, noble voice, rapid but distinct utterance and telling gestures, all accompanied with the spirit in melting tenderness, made Rickman one of the greatest pulpit orators of the mountains.

He delivered a sermon to the Western Baptist Convention, in Waynesville; in 1872, that a competent judge said exceeded the sermon of one of the most noted ministers in N. C.

But a disease, known as bronchitis, began its work upon this devoted servant, and his hitherto wonderful lungs gradually gave way.

He was afflicted for several months, during which time he grew weaker and weaker during the summer of 1874. During his latter weeks of suffering he reviewed his life carefully, examining his preaching, and was heard remark that he felt that he had preached the truth. He lingered and grew lower and lower until Oct. 3rd, 1874, when he bade adieu to earth and weeping friends and passed to the Spirit world, and his body was buried near his church he loved so well, to await the second coming of his Redeemer.

Elder Mark May.

Elder Mark May, son of Fredrick and Nellie May, was born in Yadkin county, N. C., Dec. 7th, 1812. He was married to Belinda Rearman at the age of twenty-four years. Professed faith in Christ in his twenty-seventh year, and joined the Cross Roads Baptist church, Yadkin county, and was baptized by Elder Barton Rabey, and ordained to the ministry shortly afterwards. His qualifications for the ministry were very limited; but he applied himself to the study of Theology, in which he made great advancement.

The first seventeen years of his gospel ministry, he spent in Yadkin and adjoining counties in the pastorate and missionary work. He traveled and labored for three successive years as missionary, and at the same time was pastor of four churches. In his report to the Yadkin Association, in 1847, we find that he labored 320 days; traveled 2534 miles; preached 269 sermons; baptized 185 persons; received as a compensation $147.77.

We also find that during one other year of his labors that he baptized three hundred persons. This was in the forty-fourth year of his age. About this time he moved to the western part of the State, where he lived and labored the remainder of his life except two years in Tennessee.

Duriug his ministry in Western North Carolina, he was admired as a doctrinal preacher, having but few if any equals.

He often visited Conventions, Associations, and Union meetings, where he many times charmed his hearers by his eloquent presentation of the truth as it is in Jesus.

His home for many years was in Macon county, where he was a

pattern of industry as a minister and citizen, and his name is familiar and dear to hundreds of acquaintances and brethren and sisters.

It is estimated that he baptized fifteen hundred persons during his ministry in Western North Carolina.

He was the first Clerk of the Friendship Baptist Association, now Tennessee River, as he was a member of that body for a few years.

In connection with Elder F. M. Morgan, he was engaged in a protracted meeting with his home church (Briar Town.) His last sermon was preached on Thursday before his death; text Ruth 1:16. This sermon was one of his best efforts. On Saturday, on his way to church, he was taken very ill, when kind friends took him home.

For eight hours he suffered and talked. "God be near me," he said, "My only hope is in the blood of Jesus." "My preaching is done. I was born to die, and perhaps as well now as any time," and after bidding all farewell, he died, aged 73 years, and in the ministry 46 years.

Elder Elias D. Brendle.

Elder E. D. Brendle was born in Burke county, N. C., June 30th 1814. He was brought up of Dutch parentage on a farm. He and the Brendle family resided for many years in Haywood county, N. C. He was given a common school education and taught school some in his early youth. Our subject was converted and joined the Scotts Creek Baptist church in what is now Jackson county, N. C., Sept. 9th 1845. Here Elder Brendle was ordained a Deacon, May 22nd, 1847 and subsequently ordained to the ministry of the gospel, Nov. 26th 1853. He was chosen pastor of Scotts Creek church at the time o his ordination.

Elder Brendle was married to Celinda V. Plott, daughter of Henry and Lydia Plott, Nov. 4th, 1838. His wife was born in Haywood county, N. C., June 6th, 1815. She was converted in the 22nd year of her age and joined the Waynesville Baptist church and was baptized in Richland Creek in 1837. So Elder Brendle had a good christian companion with whom to battle for the Master. They raised 7 children, son and daughters.

Elder Brendle served many of the Jackson county churches as pastor and was Moderator of the Tuckasiege Association for several sessions. As to the number of churches he aided in organizing, the number of preachers he helped ordain and persons who were baptized by him we are not informed, but his work in these particulars abound in Haywood, Macon, Jackson and Swain counties. Bryson City church was largely the work of Elder Brendle aided by others. He was pastor of Charleston church from the first, for four or five years

Our subject saw sad trouble in the loss of his first wife, which ocurred Aug. 7th, 1851, leaving him with a family of small children. n this condition of bereavement, Elder Brendle remained until the ourth Sunday in May, 1855, when he was again united in matrimoy to Miss Talitha Paris, a christian woman of good, agreeable qualiies and with whom he spent his remaining days on earth.

Our subject was a warm-hearted, industrious minister of Jesus hrist, who loved his calling, striving to understand his duty, and by is indomitable energy he acquired a good store of information in ivine things which he was fully able to deal out to his hearers in a vay not to be gainsayed. His discourses were plain and were generlly delivered with strong emotion when he warmed up in dealing ut the gospel of our great salvation. He was a strong Baptist and ften preached forcible sermons on the controverted doctrinal points eld by Baptists.

He loved his country and neighborhood and was a warm friend of ducation which he faithfully advocated.

He was a hard worker, when at home, and made the farm and rchard yield to his comfort. The Lord blessed our dear brother by vhich he procured a handsome living for himself and a good start or his children

He was very liberal in working for and contributing to the Lord's ause and his house was the home of the stranger and the Christian ilgrim.

He was humble and visited the poor. He was charitable and kind nd so filled his allotted time on earth suffering affliction for considrable time before his death, which took place, December 17, 1886.

Jno. S. Smiley.

Rev. W. H. Conner.

~~Rev. W. M. Queen.~~

W. H. Conner, son of Jacob and Massey Conner, was born in Lincoln county, N. C., April 27th, 1827. His chances for an education were not very good, but he could read and write, and by his industry he became well informed. He was married to Rachel Gibson, who made him one of the best of wives.

This happy couple were well matched and well blessed. The Lord gave them a large family of sons and daughters. In 1846 Young Conner became a citizen of Western N. C. He professed faith in Christ and was baptized into Lufty Baptist church by Elder Jacob Mingus in June, 1847. He moved his membership to Shoal Creek Baptist church in 1850, where he was licensed to preach the gospel in July 1858.

Brother Conner subsequently moved his membership to Shady Grove Baptist church about the year 1860, where he was ordained to the full work of the gospel ministry in 1861, by Elders ————

From this time forth, Elder Conner led an active life for the Master. He labored much as pastor and Evangelist in the counties of Jackson, Macon and Swain. He served two churches in Sevier county, Tennessee, as pastor, and held several revivals in that State in connection with Elder Richard Evans.

Elder Conner was also a warm friend and co-laborer with Elder E. D. Brendle with whom he did some of his most successful revival work. The churches, Lufty, Shoal Creek, Savanah and Cowee and Brush Creek, we believe, were the scenes of Elder Conner's most extensive pastorates and revivals. He was a most popular missionary to the Eastern Band of Cherokee Indians, in which place he was successful in leading many of the Indians to Christ, as the minutes of the Western N. C. Baptist Convention will show. Elder Conner dwelt a few years in Macon county in the Oak Grove neighborhood, during which time his membership was in Cowee Baptist church.

His latter years from about 1865 or 1866, were spent on the Robert Collins farm on the head of Lufty river, where he had become possessed of about 1,200 acres of land, and which was his home until death. Here about July 1885, he, Jacob like, had to part with his beloved Rachel, who was so faithful and kind and good. From his Lufty home, Elder Conner repeatedly, for different terms, served Cowee church as pastor. Here his faithful services as pastor, closed in March, 1887. On his return from a trip to Cowee about the first of March 1887, he was stricken with paralysis in the ford Deep Creek, near Bryson City, from which he died March 14th, 1887, thus ending a life of thirty years in the ministry.

The subject of our sketch had been married to Mary Burnett for more than a year prior to his decease. His loss was deeply felt by his denomination to whom he was true as steel.

Elder Conner had, during his career in the Master's work, witnessed about 1,500 professions of religion and baptized 1000 persons into the fellowship of the church.

He was hasty in temperament, tender and pathetic in sympathy with fallen man and persuasive in his appeals. By his tender, melting nature, generally bathed in tears and burning zeal of overflowing soul and aided by the good Spirit, sinners were made to cry for mercy and turn to the Savior. Many of the most useful Christians in many of the churches are among the number of his converts. He rests from his labors and his works do follow him.

JNO. S. SMILEY.

C. B. Mingus.

Rev. C. B. Mingus was the son of Ephraim and Sophia Mingus. He was born in Haywood county, N. C., on Raven's Fork of Ocone Lufty, Sept. 25th, 1823, where he was raised, educated, converted to the Lord and commenced preaching the gospel.

Our subject had a severe struggle to get loose from sin, his unbelief was so strong. But conviction deepened and he died to the love of sin and was made alive in Christ, and forthwith began to preach Christ. He first joined the Methodists but remained in that connection but a short time. He joined the Lufty Baptist church on Saturday before the third Sunday in May, 1846, and was baptized by Elder Jacob Mingus, on the third Sunday in May 1846.

Brother Mingus remained in Lufty church, where he had commenced preaching, until the third Sunday in Sept. 1848, when he removed his membership to Locust Field, near the ford of Pigeon river. He married Miss M. J. Osborne July 21st, 1858, who died July 21st, 1859, without children.

In his latter locality, brother Mingus was destined to do a great work for the Lord. He was ordained June 12th, 1847, by Elders Wm. Haynes, Thomas Henson. Josh Ammous and Jno. Haynes.

Here he served the churches as pastor for which place he was well qualified, and for a long time was the only Baptist preacher in Haywood county. Many of the noble churches of that county and some of her best Baptist preachers are the outgrowth of Elder Mingus' labors. Elder Mingus served his Association, Tuckaseige, as Moderator for several sessions, and was very popular with his people.

He lost his first wife and married Miss Rebecca A. Young, March

6th, 1864, who kindly and faithfully aided our brother to raise his dear children, and encourage him in his Master's work, for sister Mingus is truly one of the best women in Western North Carolina. Seven children make up the family.

Our brother was slow to lay hands on men for ordination, believing, as he expressed himself, that it was not necessary to ordain Elders or Bishops until some church actually needed and demanded their labors as such.

Brother Mingus faithfully served Bryson City church two years, being succeeded by Elder G. H. Church in Feb., 1890, a few months before his death. He was in bad health for twenty years, and for that length of time had been expecting his demise. He was sound, able and faithful as a preacher to the close of life, when he met death as a christian at 7:40 p. m., April 4th, 1890.

Elder Jacob Mingus.

This faithful servant was raised or partly so and did most of his work as a minister while on Oconee Lufty and a member of said church.

He served Lufty as a pastor for a period of about twenty years. He served Cold Spring for three months as pastor in 1851, soon after which time he moved to Missouri and died in a few years.

Elder Jacob Stillwell.

This brother was ordained in Lufty and did work for the Master in some parts of Western North Carolina and removed, we think, to Texas. He was one among the first preachers in the territory of Tennessee River Baptist Association.

Elder Young Ammons.

This aged minister of Jesus was entitled to a sketch in our History, but the writer was unable to obtain necessary information for such.

Young Ammons was a brother to the noted Joshua Ammons, of Macon county, N. C., and of one of the best families in the western part of the state.

We think that he was born in Buncombe county, N. C., and was over four score years old at his death, which took place about the year 1887, dying as the christian dies. We think he commenced his ministry in Tennessee and was in that work forty or fifty years.

The closing days of his life were spent in Panther Creek Baptist church of Tennessee River Association where he lived as a dutiful citizen.

He raised a large family of children and filled a long life of trials and struggles, as many do, and finally and patiently obeyed the summons of his master to rest from his labors, and fell asleep with his fathers to awake to the last trump.

The Writer's Humble Experience.

The writer, son and oldest child of Rev. J. M. and Annie Smiley, was born in Rutherford county, N. C., ten miles east of Rutherfordton on the waters of Robenson's Creek, Nov. 11, 1843.

His father moved to Watauga creek in Macon county, N. C., in December, 1845, in which settlement he entered his son into school in the first part of his sixth year. But little schooling fell to his lot, being about twelve months in the log school house of common county schools, during his single life.

After marriage the writer attended Normal Schools for the benefit of teachers about ten weeks, which, added to that of his home improvement, makes up the amount of his education. So it may be truly said that his education is limited to a Common School English education. The writer was brought up on the farm and taught to till the earth for a living.

He volunteered as a soldier in the Confederate service in Company E. 39 N. C Regiment in Dec. 1861, and served in that command and Thomas' Legion until the war closed, April 1865.

He was not so much exposed to bullets as some of his comrades in arms, owing to assignments by his very worthy Col., David Coleman, who made him a fifer of the regiment, in consequence of which he was not required to bear arms.

He was never exposed to but two noted engagements, the eight days siege of Jackson, Mississippi in July, 1863, and the celebrated battle of Chickamauga, Ga.. 19th and 20th of September, 1863. Here, in this battle, under Gen. Braxton Bragg, providence provided for his escape from much of the deadly storm of battle by his brave Col onel detailing him to take care of his horse during the conflict, specially charging the writer not to expose himself to the battle. God took care of the unworthy writer through all the war struggle, and he has been spared, he hopes, for some good purpose, while eight of his intimate associates and schoolmates were slain in battle and two of them seriously wounded.

He married Happuch Matilda, daughter of John S. and Martha A. Gibson, July 26th, 1866.

Starting life in the common poverty of the times, he took up the honorable occupations of the farm and that of teaching school. While he has been poor in purse, he has been made rich in blessed gifts from the good Lord, he and his dear wife having been given six sons and six daughters.

He gained an humble hope in Christ near Clinton, Tennessee, in April, 1862, and joined the Cowee Baptist church, Macon county, N. C., January 1863, and was baptized in McGaha prong of Cowee creek, by Elder Merritt Rickman. His church membership was transferred to Cold Spring Baptist church in Feb. 1865.

He had impressions to exercise in public in preachidg not very long after he joined, but did not make such an attempt until September, 1871.

His first text was in Psalms 62:8.

Long, and halting between two opinions, he often tried to wave the ministerial duty by studying on politics, desiring much to become a Statesman, and was twice defeated for office in his native county, which about mortified all his hopes and political aspirations, resulting in an end of those inward longings, which was doubtless for his religious good. Meanwhile, he continued occasional exercises by way of preaching and after being urged and advised by many of his brethren and sisters, ministers and others, he finally submitted and was licensed by Cold Spring church in July 1876.

He believes in a divine call to the ministry, and whenever his faith grew a little weak, or when the impressions relaxed to some extent, as they sometimes did, or when he would preach and did not witness results immediately, he was often led to conclude that he had undertaken the wrong task, and then was ready to quit preaching, for he never doubted the reality of the Christian religion, or the divine call or impressions to the ministry, but he has often doubted himself. Having become connected with Charleston Baptist church in 1878, a church then in its infancy, being about a year old when he joined it, he was induced by pastor, E. D. Brendle and others, to accept the office of deacon to which he was soon ordained.

Now he hoped that he might content himself and turn his attention to the deacon's duties and be no more a preacher, but this made no excuse and so he continued to try to preach. Time and again had he been spoken to in regard to ordination to the ministry, but would not consent until after he went before an Examining Board of ministers of Tuckaseige Baptist Association whose business it was, not to ordain, but to encourage young gifts, and to recommend them to their churches for ordination when they found them qualified for the divine work. This, which took place in Aug. 1880, at Coweta church, was one of the most strengthening props, and the examination of those worthy brethren and fathers in the ministry, E. D. Brendle and I. D. Wright, and the noble hearted young Elder, S. H. Harrington was the turning point of his resolves touching the ministry. His christian experience, divine call to preach and literary attainments, particularly, his knowledge of the doctrine of the Bible, all proving satisfactory to the Board, led him to fully decide to do his duty by continuing in the ministry and to submit to ordination when his church saw proper to set him forward, and upon a call of the Charleston church he was ordained to the full work of the Christian ministry by a presbytery, consisting of Elders E. D. Brendle, W. H. Conner, A. A. Justice, J. M. Smiley and J. U. Salts, December 19th, 1881. By the act of his ordination, the writer was still more fully strengthened and built up in soul to follow the Master, Jesus, wherever he says go, as opportunity permits; and only in duty is he blessed, and a gracious Savior and Comforter has dispelled many of his former doubts and fears, but he has learned not to trust in the flesh nor the will of man. He has aided in organizing a few churches and ordaining a few deacons, ministers, and has served as pastor about six years, but it seems that most of his religious usefulness is yet to come, if come it ever does.

He was Clerk of Cold Spring church a few years and was also Clerk of Tennessee River Baptist Association in 1872 and 1873, and filled the same again, in 1883 and 1884. He has served as messenger to the Western North Carolina Baptist Convention for six years at different periods, commencing his first service thus at Cowee in September 1876. He loves the Baptist institutions, churches, Associations, schools and periodicals, and always labors for their upbuilding and encourrgement from his scanty purse, pen and tongue. He is also deeply impressed with missionary sentiments, believing it to be the high privilege and duty of the church and ministry to support the gospel at home and send it abroad so as to bring the lost sinner and heathen to Christ. He was chosen the first historian of his Association in 1876, and has labored in getting up this volume for about nine years at intervals, having commenced the work in January 1877.

As teacher of schools, the writer commenced in August, 1867, and taught a few weeks, followed in teaching a few weeks in 1868. But it was not until Swain county was organized that his teaching career took permanent shape. He commenced teaching in Charleston District in the first public schools of Swain county, N. C., Oct. 9, 1871, and has taught in different public schools of the county for sixteen years. He taught a school in Rabun, Ga., in 1875. Summing up his school lists of different pupils they run to about six or seven hundred. Without solicitation on his part, the writer was chosen County Examiner by the Board of Education of Swain county, N. C., in July, 1878, took the United States census in Nantahala township in June 1880, and was chosen the first County Superintendent of Public Instruction of Swain county, June 6, 1881, to which place he, always without soliciting on his part, his worthy county authorities upon whom the election devolved, five times chose him in succession. The work of the superintendency has been blessed in his hands, but it was not executed without some severe trials and arduous duties. He has instructed about 200 teachers, or students for such, in eight Teachers' Institutes and examined about the same number of teachers and visited the public schools of the county seven years, traveled more than 1,400 miles on such duties, and addressed and encouraged about 400 pupils.

The educational life of the writer is interwoven with the history of Swain county, N. C., from its existence, being now twenty years, ten of which he served as Examiner, County Superintendent and Secretary of the Board of Education, and while he realizes his weakness and shortcomings, he can but feel some degree of pride in his educational history, and humbly hopes that upon the humble foundation he has thus been enabled to lay for the dear children of his county, that a far brighter day and greater degree of prosperity may dawn upon the succeeding schools and those entrusted with their guidance.

REVIEW OF TWELVE MINISTERS' LIVES IN WESTERN NORTH CAROLINA

Humphrey Posey, aged 66 years, in the ministry 42 years;
David Elder, aged about 56 years, in the ministry about 20 years;
James Kimzey, aged 66 years, in the ministry 40 years;
Samuel Gibson, aged 83 years, in the ministry 44 years;
Merritt Rickman, aged 62 years, in the ministry 38 years;
Allen Ammons, aged 60 years, in the ministry 34 years;
I T. S. Sherrill, aged 74 years, in the ministry 44 years;
C. B. Mingus, aged 66 years, in the ministry 44 years;
E. D. Brendle, aged 72 years, in the ministry 33 years;
Mark May, aged 73 years, in the ministry 46 years;
W. H. Conner, aged 60 years, in the ministry 30 years;
J. M. Smiley, aged 60 years, in the ministry 25 years;

The average ages of the above named brethren, without using the fractional parts, was 63 years; average terms in the ministry during life, 36 years; average ages at commencement in the ministry was 27 years.

By the foregoing, we conclude that the average life of a minister is about sixty and the average term in the ministry is about thirty five years.

Miscellaneous Supplement,

CONTAINING

"DISTINCTIVE BAPTIST MARKS," "ESSENTIAL ELEMENTS OF A CHURCH," "BAPTIST ASSOCIATIONS—WHAT THEY ARE," CONSTITUTION OF THE ASSOCIATION AND OF W. N. C. CONVENTION, SOUTHERN B. CONVENTION, DELIBERATIVE ASSEMBLY GUIDE, ETC.

DISTINCTIVE BAPTIST MARKS.

1. The Bible is the sole and sufficient rule in all matters of religion —to the exclusion of human traditions.

2. A regenerate membership—to the exclusion of irresponsible children and confessedly unsaved persons from our churches.

3. Each church is an independent body, owning Christ only as Head and with only executive powers—to the exclusion of all human authorities, ecclesiastical powers in "Councils," "Synods," and the like, and of all human legislation.

4. The equality of the members—to the exclusion of all grades, distinctions and dignities, which are the creations of human pride.

5. The equality of the ministry—to the exclusion of all human masteries and chief ministers and clerical orders introduced by Rome and her copyists.

6. The ordinances, in number order, subject, administrator and symbolism, kept as delivered in solemn charge by Christ and his Apostles.

ESSENTIAL ELEMENTS OF A CHURCH.

I. Scriptural Origin.—By Christ himself while on earth. Dan. 2:44; Matt. 3.2; 16:18, and 18:17.

II. Scriptural Polity.—Not Presbyterial nor Episcopal, but a pure Democracy, Government in the hands of the people, and not of a privileged class. Matt. 18:17; Acts 1:26; 6: 1-8; 15:22, and chapters 5 and 6 of 1. Cor.

III. Scriptural Membership.—Terms of: 1, Regeneration, evidenced by repentance and faith; and 2, Baptism, immersion in water by an authorized administrator. Mk. 16:15; John 3:3-and 5; Acts 8:35 and Acts 16.

IV. Scriptural Officers—1. The Spiritual Ministry, variously called Bishops, Elders, etc., and 2. The Temporal Ministry, Deacons. No grades in the Ministry. 1. Pet. 5:1; 1. Tim. 3:1, Acts 20:17 and 28. Qualifications for only these two classes of officers given by Paul in Tim. and Titus.

V. Scriptural Ordinances.—Immersion, in water, of a believer by the authority of a Gospel Church. Matt. 3:13—end, and Acts 8:35—end, and Rom. 6:3-5. Lord's Supper, as a memento of the manner of Christ's death, approachable only by members of Gospel Churches, as above described, section III Luke 22:19 and 20; Matt. 28:19 and 20; Acts 2:37—42 and 1. Cor. 11:23-26.

VI. Scriptural Doctrines. —All Scriptural doctrines.— All Scriptural doctrines included, and all human traditions excluded Rev. 22:18 and 19; Mk. 7:7 and 13 13; 11. Tim. 3:16. Heb. 13:9 and 11. Tim. 3:16. Heb. 13:9 and 11. Tim. 1:13.

Scriptural History.—Continuous from the days of the Apostles. Dan. 2:44; Matt. 16:18. Testimony of Pedo-baptists confirms the same. A Wilderness Epoch. Rev. 12:14. Not "Apostolic Succession," or any succession at all, strictly speaking but merely this: That the cardinal principles and practices of Baptists are of New Testament origin and that they have never been extinct at any period of the Christian era.

BAPTIST ASSOCIATIONS.—WHAT THEY ARE.

Baptist Associations are Baptist brotherhoods of churches organized for the purpose of united efforts in the work of extending the Redeemer's kingdom in the world.

They are also Advisory Councils to advise for the general good of the cause among the churches whose servants they are, but they have no coercive power; and consequently can pass no laws binding upon the churches.

Associations are creatures of the churches, made up of messengers chosen from each in such numbers as the churches may choose, and should always consist of all the ministers belonging to the churches, especially, and the deacons and others whom the churches may think suitable councellors. Churches may or may not send messengers to an Association as each church is an independent body accountable to no one but Christ, but when good advice is given by an Association churches should regard it. Associations have no power to hear appeals from the churches as no appeal can be taken from a church, so also, in regard to ordaining ministers, receiving, dismissing and disciplining members of the church, they have no power further than to advise in such cases A Baptist Association has the right to encourage good order and sound doctrine and to withdraw from churches which deviate from these.

THE AUTHOR.

CONSTITUTION OF TENNESSEE RIVER ASSOCIATION.

ARTICLE 1. This association shall be called the Tennessee River Association.

ART. 2. The association shall be composed of male members chosen by the respective churches in our union, duly sent to represent them in the Association, and upon their producing certificates from their respective churches, certifying their appointment, their churches having complied with this constitution, they shall be entitled to seats in the body.

ART. 3. In the certificates shall be expressed the number baptized, received by letter, restored, dismissed, excluded and died since last Association. Also the number of teachers and pupils in Sunday schools, the time of prayer meeting, amount of. their pastor's salary, his name, their postoffice, the number of ordained ministers and licentiates, the contribution, the total number of members.

ART. 4. This Association shall have no power to lord it over God's heritage, nor shall it infringe upon any of the internal rights of any church in the union; but this shall not be construed to prevent the Association from encouraging a sound and able ministry, or discouraging an ignorant, unsound and disorderly one.

ART. 5. This Association shall have a moderator, clerk, historian and treasurer; the moderator and clerk to be elected by absolute majorities. Historian and Treasurer in any way the body may direct.

ART. 6. This Association shall have the right to determine what churches shall be admitted as members of the body.

ART. 7. This Association shall have the right to withdraw her fellowship from any church for not complying with her constitution, or for violating the orthodox principles of the gospel.

ART. 8. The moderator shall always have the Articles of Faith, Constitution and Rules of Decorum at the meetings of the body.

ART. 9. This constitution may be altered or amended by a two-thirds vote of the members present.

ORDER OF BUSINESS.

THURSDAY.

1. Singing, prayer and introductory, recess.
2. Singing and prayer, call to order, appoint reading clerk.
3. Call roll of churches and enroll delegates.
4. Elect officers.
5. Appoint committees, as follows:
    1. Religious Exercises.
    2. Obituaries and Changes.
    3. Time and Place, Introductory, etc.

4. Temperance.
5. Home Missions.
6. Foreign Missions.
7. Conventional Missions.
8. Education.
9. Sunday Schools.
10. Periodicals.
11. Finance.
12. Minister's Names and Addresses.
13. Miscellany.

FRIDAY AND SATURDAY.

1. Singing or reading and prayer.
2. Call roll, read minutes, etc.
3. Call for correspondents.
4. Call for report of committees in order.
5. Call for report of historian.
6. Call for report of treasurer.
7. Arrange Sabbath preaching, collection, etc.
8. Appoint delegates to Western Baptist Convention.
9. Instruct clerks as to the minutes, etc.
10. Miscellany, resolutions, etc.
11. Read minutes and closing exercises.

CONSTITUTION OF THE WESTERN NORTH CAROLINA BAPTIST CONVENTION.

ARTICLE I.

This body shall be called the Western North Carolina Baptist Convention, and shall hold its meetings annually and at such times and places as shall be appointed at previous meeting.

ARTICLE II.

The object of this Convention shall be: The distribution of the Holy Scriptures among the destitute; the sustentation of Home, Foreign and Conventional Missions and Church building; the education of the poor young men, called of God to the Gospel ministry; the fostering of Baptist institutions of learning within its bounds; Sabbath-schools; the dissemination of religious literature and temperance.

ARTICLE III.

The funds appropriated for these objects shall be kept distinct from each other and faithfully applied according to the desire of the contributors.

ARTICLE IV.

By paying into the treasury, annually, the sum of $5, any Baptist church, association, society, or individual, shall be entitled to one representative, who is a member in good standing of a Baptist church, and for the sum of $30 the representative shall be constituted a life member.

ARTICLE V.

This body shall annually elect, by ballot, a President, 1st and 2nd Vice Presidents, Recording Secretary, Treasurer, Auditor, and Historian. Provided, however, that all officers after the President, may be elected *viva voce.* All officers shall remain in office till their successors are chosen.

ARTICLE VI.

It shall be the duty of the President to preside at all meetings of the Convention, sign all orders; and in the absence of the President, this duty shall devolve on one of the Vice Presidents, according to the order of appointment. The Secretary shall preserve a faithful record of all the proceedings of the body, and conduct the correspondence therefor. The treasurer shall give bond and approved security for the faithful discharge of his duty, and shall hold all the funds of the Convention subject to its orders, and shall submit an annual report of all his receipts and expenditures, the same to be audited and published in the minutes. The Historian shall keep a complete file of the minutes of this body, and shall record, in a book kept for the purpose, facts, historical, biographical, and incidental, and whatever is likely to be of special use to the future Historian, and shall read his record annually in open Convention, which when approved, shall be considered authentic history.

ARTICLE VII.

This body shall at each annual meeting, appoint the following Boards: A Board of Conventional and Sunday School Missions of 23 members 10 of whom shall reside in Asheville, 7 of whom shall constitute a quorum to transact business, located at Asheville; a Board of Ministerial Education of 11 members, 3 of whom shall constitute a quorum to transact business located at Asheville to whom shall be committed the respective departments of the Convention's work during its recess. These Boards shall each present to the annual meeting of the Convention a well digested report of the work in charge.

ARTICLE VIII.

This body, through its proper officers, will co-operate with the boards of the Southern Baptist Convention in the prosecution of its common work.

ARTICLE IX.

This Convention may employ any agency by which the objects contemplated in its organization may be accomplished.

ARTICLE X.

Any alteration may be made in this Constitution by a vote of two-thirds of its members present at any annual meeting.

ARTICLE XI.

This body shall be governed by "Mell's Manual of Parliamentary Practice."

ARTICLE XII.

Whenever the minutes of the Convention are printed a copy of this Constitution shall be printed therein.

ARTICLE XIII.

The fiscal year of this Convention shall close on this the 15th day of October, and the Secretary's and Treasurer's reports shall bear date accordingly.

CONSTITUTION.

We, the delegates from missionary societies, churches and other religious bodies of the Baptist denomination in various parts of the United States, met in convention in the city of Augusta, Georgia, for the purpose of carrying into effect the benevolent intentions of our constituents, by organizing a plan for eliciting, combining and directing the energies of the whole denomination in one sacred effort for the propagation of the gospel, agree to the following rules or fundamental principles:

Art. I. This body shall be styled the "Southern Baptist Convention."

Art. II. It shall be the design of this Convention to promote foreign and domestic missions, and other important objects connected with the Redeemer's kingdom, and to combine for this purpose such portions of the Baptist denomination in the United States as may desire a general organization for Christian benevolence, which shall fully respect the independence and equal rights of the churches.

Art. III. The Convention shall consist (1) of brethren who contribute funds, or are delegated by Baptist bodies contributing funds for the regular work of the Convention, on the basis of one delegate for every $250 actually paid into the treasuries of the Boards during fiscal year, ending the 30th day of April next preceding the meeting of the Convention; (2) of one representative from each of the District Associations which co-operate with this Convention, provided that such representative be formally elected by his District Association and his election certified to the Secretaries of the Convention, either in writing or by a copy of the printed Minutes; and (3) of one representative for every $500 collected and expended conjointly with either of the Boards of this Convention, by any State Convention or General Association.

Art. IV. The officers of this Convention shall be a President, four Vice-Presidents, a Treasurer, an Auditor, who shall in event of the death or disability of the Treasurer, act as such officer, and two Secretaries, who shall be elected at each annual meeting, and hold their offices until a new election; and the officers of the Convention shall be, each by virtue of his office, members of the several Boards.

ART. V. The Convention shall elect at each annual meeting as many Boards of Managers as in its judgement will be necessary for carrying out the benevolent objects it may determine to promote—all which Boards may continue in office until a new election. Each Board shall consist of a President, Vice-President, Secretaries, Treasurer, Auditor, and fifteen other members, seven of whom, including one or more of the officers, shall form a quorum for the transaction of business. To each Board shall be committed, during the recess of the Convention the entire management of all the affairs relating to the objects with whose interest it shall be charged, all of which management shall be in strict accordance with the constitutional provisions adopted by this Convention, and such other instructions as may be given from time to time. Each Board shall have power to make such compensation to its Secretaries and Treasurer as it may think right, fill the vacancies occurring in its own body, and enact its own By-laws.

ART. VI. The Treasurer of each Board shall faithfully account for all moneys received by him, keep a regular entry of all receipts and disbursements, and make report of them to the Convention whenever it shall be in session, and to his Board as often as required. He shall also, on entering upon the duties of his office, give competent security to the President of the Board for all the stock and funds committed to his care. His books shall be open at all times to the inspection of any member of the Convention and of his Board. No moneys shall be paid out of any of the treasuries of the Board but by an order from that Board from whose treasury the money is to be drawn, which order shall be signed by the presiding officer.

ART. VII. The Corresponding Secretary of the several Boards shall maintain intercourse by letter with such individuals or public bodies as the interest of their respective bodies may require. Copies of all such communications, with their answers, if any, shall be kept by them on file.

ART. VIII. The Recording Secretaries of the several Boards shall keep a fair record of their proceedings, and of such other documents as may be committed to them for the purpose.

ART. IX. All the officers, Boards, Missionaries and Agents appointed by the Convention, or by any of its Boards, shall be members of some regular church in the union with the churches composing this Convention.

ART. X. Missionaries appointed by any of the Boards of this Convention must, previous to their appointment, furnish evidence of genuine piety, fervent zeal in their Master's cause, and talents which fit them for the service for which they offer themselves.

ART. XI. The bodies and individuals composing this Convention shall have the right to specify the object or objects to which their contributions shall be applied. But when no such specification is made, the Convention will make the appropriation at its own discretion.

ART. XII. The Convention shall hold its meetings annually, but extra meetings may be called by the President, with the approbation of any one of the Boards of Managers. A majority of the attending delegates shall not be necessary to form a quorum for the transaction of business. The President, or in the event of his death, any of the Vice-Presidents of the Convention, may, at the request of two of its Boards, postpone or alter the place of meeting of the Convention, when it may be deemed by him inexpedient to convene at the time or place appointed.

ART. XIII. Any alterations which experience shall dictate may be made in these Articles by a vote of two-thirds of the members present at any annual meeting of the Convention.

BY-LAWS.

Impressed with the obligation resting on the Convention to endeavor more energetically and systematically to elicit, combine and direct the energies of the whole denomination in one sacred effort for the propagation of the gospel, we adopt the following By-laws:

1. That the Boards of the Convention be directed to form the closest possible connection with State Boards, where such exist, in such way as shall be mutually agreeable, and in other cases to secure such agency as each of the Boards may deem best, in both cases providing for necessary expenses incurred.

2. That the Secretaries of the Boards of the Convention be instructed to secure frequent distribution of information relating to their work by means of newspapers, tracts, leaflets and otherwise, as may be found expedient among the mass of the people.

3. That the committee on the nomination of New Boards be instructed to nominate, as Vice-Presidents of Boards, men known to be identified with the interests of the Convention, and of their own State Boards, and unless special reasons exist to the contrary, men who make effort to attend the sessions of the Convention. These Vice-Presidents shall be expected to co-operate with the Boards, both giving and receiving suggestions as to the work to be done, and they also shall be expected to present at the next session of the Convention, a report in writing of what they had been requested to do, and of the way in which they have complied with these requests, with any suggestions they may have to offer as to the condition and needs of their respective fields. It shall be the duty of each Secretary, in due time, to furntsh the Vice-Presidents of his Board with suitable blanks for such reports, and to call their attention to this article, and to make any proper effort to secure the due preparation of these reports. In case any Vice-Prasident appointed is unable or unwilling to comply with the requests herein mentioned, it shall be the duty of the Board, if possible, to find some person who can, and request him to do so; and furthermore, the Vice-President for each State shall be desired, as speedily as possible, to prepare a roll of the associations, churches and Sunday schools in that State, to be used for the distribution of information, and to ascertain as far as possible which of the churches and Sunday-schools are contributing to the funds of the Board and

the annual amounts, and to make systematic effort each year to increase the number and amount of such contributions.

4. The Boards shall report at each session of the Convention what special efforts they have been able to make toward carrying out the object of these By-laws.

5. Immediately after the reading of the reports of the Boards, each year, a committee of five shall be appointed, to whom shall be referred so much of these reports as pertains to the carrying out of the By-laws, and also the reports of the Vice-Presidents.

6. That these By-laws may be altered at any time by a majority vote, except on the last day of the Convention.

DELIBERATIVE ASSEMBLY GUIDE,

BY

REV. JOHN S. SMILEY,

Swain, N. C.,

ALL IN A NUT SHELL.

ADAPTED TO ALL

Practical Purposes,

In Mass Meetings, Churches, Associations, Societies, Legislative Bodies, etc.

1892.

PARLIAMENTARY.

PARLIAMEMTARY RULES, GOVERNING DELIBERATIVE BODIES IN GENERAL.

1. DELIBERATIVE BODIES are organized assemblies of persons convened to act upon questions legally presented to them according to the principles and forms sanctioned by usage.

2. In deliberative bodies the members are on an equality, and the officers are but the instruments and agents of them.

There are two classes of deliberative bodies. 1. PERMANENT. 2. OCCASIONAL.

Permanent deliberative bodies have no constituencies, but maintain the relation at will, or for life; such as churches, local societies, the House of Peers in England, etc.

Occasional deliberative bodies have constituencies, such as District Associations, Conventions, State Legislatures and the House of Representatives in the Congress of the United States, political meetings, etc.

All deliberative bodies must have a presiding and recording officer.

Presiding officers have different titles in English and American Parliamentary Law, according to the customs of the kinds of bodies over which they preside. President is the title of the presiding officer of the U. S. Senate, and some of the State Senates, and Speaker is the title of the presiding officer in the House of Representatives of the U. S., and of the several States.

Moderator is the title of the presiding officer of a Baptist church, Union Meeting, Association, Synods and Assemblies of the Presbyterians and of a Town Meeting in Massachusetts.

President of some Baptist Conventions is the title of the presiding officer and Bishop, the presiding officer in a Methodist Conference, an Episcopal Diocese, etc. Chairman, is used sometimes in mass meetings and always in Committees and very often in that of County Boards, Boards of Missions, etc.

QUALIFICATIONS OF A PRESIDING OFFICER.

The presiding officer of an assembly should well understand parliamentary law and be fully able to preside so as to reflect credit on himself and his assembly.

He should seldom if ever engage in debate as a partisan on a general question. His duties are to keep the assembly in working order, to submit such questions for decision as may properly come before the body in order, and to decide points of order and rule the members to the same. But to succeed well and sustain the proper respect of members, the presiding officer should, on most principal questions, act the part of a disinterested umpire.

When the hour fixed for the meeting of the assembly arrives, the presiding officer should take the chair, or seat intended for the chair, and call the body to order, and call the atteniion of the body to the business before it.

The recording officer of an assembly should be well able to commit to writing the proceedings as they are transacted. He should be a ready penman, quick of perception and be fully able to keep a true minute or journal of the body. He should always furnish the chairmen of committees, belonging to the assembly for which he is recording, with a list of their colleagues, as they are appointed. The recording officer of deliberative bodies is either called Clerk or Secretary.

The title is that of Clerk in legislative assemblies, churches, Union meetings, Associations, etc.. and Secretary in religious and political conventions and some other societies.

In the absence of special rules to the contrary, it is the duty of the Clerk, or Secretary of former session to call his assembly, upon the opening of a new session, in case the former presiding officer or officers are absent to order and occupy the chair until a presiding officer may be provided: In such cases a chairman-protempore is chosen to act for the time until properly organized.

PRIVILEGES OF MEMBERS OF DELIBERATIVE BODIES.

The members of a deliberative body are upon an equality and each have a right to occupy the floor in debate. To obtain the floor to make a motion or introduce a resolution, or to speak upon any question, a member must first get the recognition of the presiding officer by rising to his feet and addressing the presiding officer with the proper title. If two or more rise at the same time, the chair must name the one to speak first. In all discussions, it is the duties of members to follow or keep to the subject and to avoid personalities, or an irritable manner of speech. Any member may keep the floor so long as he keeps in the bounds of reason or observes good order.

ORDER OF DEBATE.

It is not in order to make a speech when there is no question legitimately before the assembly.

The way to get questions before an assembly is by motion or resolution which must always have a second and no question is debatable until stated by the presiding officer after which it is open to all members equally alike for discussion.

HOW A VOTE IS TAKEN UPON A QUESTION.

The presiding officer rises and after stating the question says:

"All in favor of the motion, (or resolution) say Aye;" when the Ayes have been taken he reverses the vote by saying, "All who are opposed to it say, "No," after which he announces the result of the vote by saying, "It has carried,' or "It has failed," as the case may be, and the vote is with the voice. In cases of election of officers of deliberative bodies, (especially permanent officers,) the vote should always be by ballot.

ORGANIZATION.

Organization of constituent deliberative bodies, when first brought into existence and before they have officers existing and also where former officers are absent whose duty it is to call them to order and serve in official capacity until permanent organization is effected, may be organized in this way:

The assembly or meeting having met at the appointed time and place it becomes the right and duty of any member to rise and move the appointment of some one to preside until permanent organization is completed, which motion having been seconded should immediately be put to the house by the mover, and if the motion thus made carries, then it is the duty of the person thus selected to take the chair at once and preside. All other temporary officers, especially a clerk or secretary, must also be provided, and so it is the duty of the person now presiding to call the attention of the body to that fact and let them be chosen in the same way as the temporary presiding officer was chosen.

The usual exercises in opening and organizing constituent deliberative bodies, is the opening address introductory to the work, devotion, etc., after which the members are called upon for credentials. The best method to insure accurate work is for the chair to appoint reading clerks to read papers from the bodies represented in the order named, which when completed to the satisfaction of the body brings on the election of permanent officers as the next step; and the election of the presiding and recording officers should always be by ballot and the persons elected should receive a majority of all the votes cast before declared elected.

A deliberative assembly is not completely organized until its appropriate committees are appointed. Any number of standing committees may be provided for by an assembly and to these certain leading questions or business may be assigned upon which it is their duty to consider and report to their assemblies in the best way.

APPOINTMENT OF COMMITTEES.

The appointment of committees, when not otherwise ordered by the assembly, devolves upon the presiding officer every time; and when a committee is raised by order of the assembly, if the order does not include the number and the persons of whom it is to consist, it is the prerogative of the presiding officer to fill the blanks without further hesitation.

A wise discretion must be used in appointing committees, from the fact that they are the business heads and motive machinery of an assembly.

Committees usually consist of an indefinite number of persons, generally exceeding two, but they should never consist of less than three, and seldom exceed three persons; and no person should be assigned to duty on more than one committee at the same time.

COMMITTEE OF THE WHOLE.

Sometimes it becomes necessary for an assembly to resolve itself into a *Committee of the Whole* to consider measures of such pressing importance as not to be satisfactorily considered and matured otherwise.

When it is desired to become a committee of the whole, some member moves that the assembly do now resolve itself into a *Committee of the Whole*, and this motion being sustained by a second is put to the house by the presiding officer which when carried requires the presiding officer to call some one to the chair to preside over the *Committee of the Whole* and the assembly now considers the matter in hand until satisfactory progress is reached, when it is the duty of some one to move that the committee of the whole do rise and report progress to the assembly. If this motion prevails, the presiding officer of the body assumes duties at the point where he left off when the body went into the *Committee of the Whole.*

MOTIONS AND RESOLUTIONS.

When a deliberative assembly expresses itself upon any question, it is done in the form of motions and resolutions, and but one principal question can be legally brought before an assembly at the same time; consequently, the presiding officer should rule out any other separate or independent motion or resolution, until the one under consideration is disposed of.

The following are all the kinds of motions and questions usually resorted to in parliamentary law.

Every question has what is termed a principal motion, and the following subsiding motions may be made during the consideration of a main proposition:

1. To lie on the table;
2. Indefinite postponement;
3. Previous question;
4. Definite postponement;
5. Amendments;
6. Commitment.

And to these we add the motion to reconsider, but this motion can not be moved by any one unless he voted in the affirmative and it is made only to bring up again, for reconsideration, a question that has been passed upon.

There are certain other questions which sometimes arise during the proceedings of an assembly which must be decided at once as they always affect the deliberations of an assembly; these are called Incidental Questions. They are:

1. Questions of order;
2. Reading papers;

3. Withdrawal of a motion ;

4. Suspension of a rule.

There are also other questions which supercede any other principal motion or any of its appendages and may interrupt these at any stage of the proceedings, and the questions which thus supercede are called *Privileged Questions*. They are :

1. Orders of the day ;
2. Questions of privilege ;
3. Adjournment.

The following motions are not debatable and must always be decided without debate :

1. The previous question ;
2. The main question, when the previous question has been seconded by the house ;
3. To lie on the table ;
4. Definite postponement ;
5. Motions to read papers ;
6. Motions to suspend the rules ;
7. Motions to adjourn.

Motions which supercede or supplant others, motion to lie on the table takes precedence of all other subsiary questions, but it is subordinate to all three of the privileged questions.

How motions accumulate sometimes, by superceding and suspending one another for the time : (1) There is a principal motion pending ; (2) a motion is made to amend ; (3) another motion is made to amend the amendment ; (4) a proposition is made to commit ; (5) a point of order is raised ; (6) a question of privilege is raised ; (7) a motion is made to adjourn.

The proper mode of proceeding in such cases is to put the question first on the motion to adjourn. If that be decided in the negative, then settle the question of privilege; decide the point of order ; then put the question on the motion to commit. If the assembly refuse to commit, the questions are to be taken on the amendments in reverse order, and finally on the principal motion amended or unamended.

THE EFFECTS OF SUBSIDIARY MOTIONS WHEN CARRIED.

To lie on the table ranks all subsidiary questions and when carried it removes from the assembly the principal motion with all its appendages for the time.

When a motion to take from the table prevails, it revives the principal motion with all other appendages attached to it in the exact form it was in before it was tabled.

To postpone to a time definite is subordinate to lie on the table, but it is of the same grade with all the other subsidiary motions, except to amend to which it is superior, and cannot be suppressed by them. Postponement to a time definite when carried in the affirmative, makes the question a privileged one for that time. If decided in the negative it leaves the question before the assembly as it was before the motion to postpone was made; and it cannot be moved a second time. It is susceptible of amendment. It is not in order to speak to the merits of a question when postponement is under consideration, but simply to speak on the time to which the postponement proposed is in order.

MOTIONS TO SUPPRESS.

To cut off discussion and bring on a direct vote, the previous question is used. When a member calls for the previous question, the presiding officer says: "Shall the call for the previous question be seconded?" If this carries in the affirmative, the second step and question by the chair is, "Shall the main question be now put?" Third and lastly, "Shall the principal motion be adopted by the house?" The previous question has supremacy over a motion to amend, but is subordinate to lie on the table. It is of the same grade with the other subsidiary questions, viz: to postpone and to commit, and when either of them is pending it is not in order to move it.

To evade a direct vote on the merits of a question, indefinite postponement is used, and when it prevails, the proposition thus postponed cannot be renewed during the session.

COMMITMENT.

It is in order to commit to a standing committee or a select committee, but if the motion to commit comes up in two forms the vote is taken on committing to the standing committee first. Commitment is of the same grade as postponement and previous question.

APPEALS FROM THE DECISIONS OF THE CHAIR.

Any member may appeal to the house from the decision of the presiding officer on points of order and the chair shall immediately take a vote on the question which vote shall settle the dispute.

POWERS AND DUTIES OF DELIBERATIVE BODIES WITH REGARD TO ENFORCING ORDER.

Every assembly must have good discipline in order to maintain its dignity and to succeed successfully with its business: thus it becomes the duty of every officer and member to conform to the established rules of moral right and usages of business. It is the duty of presiding officers to reprove for disorder and in cases of persistent violation on the part of a member, it is his duty to call the attention of the assembly to the fact, naming the offender and the offense, and the house should take the case in hand and deal with the offense according to the merits or demerits of the case. But in case of punishment for disorder in deliberative bodies, no penalty can be inflicted by them further than to unseat and deprive the guilty parties of the privileges of the assembly.

Any member may raise a question of order, calling the attention of the chair to it, and when stated the chair accepts or regrets according to his judgment in the case.

AMENDMENTS.

This is the form of question when it is desired to alter a principal proposition, and every amendment is itself subject to amendment, but there is a limit to these kind of questions beyond which we cannot go. We cannot amend an amended amendment.

Putting questions to a vote when motions to amend are to be voted upon are on this wise: First the question on the amendment to the amendment, when there are such pending; Second on the amendment as amended, and finally on the principal proposition as amended, but if all the amendments be voted down then the question will be standing in original form to be voted on. There are three ways to effect amendments, viz: (1) by adding words; (2) by striking out; (3) by striking out and inserting words.

Reconsideration, when it carries, brings the question to be reconsidered before the assembly as it was before voted upon. A motion to reconsider can only be made by those who voted in the affirmative on the proposition desired to be opened for consideration again.

ADJOURNMENT.

A motion simply to adjourn, without specifying time, supercedes all other questions, and must be put by the chair, but it can be voted down if the body is not ready for it.

ROLL CALL, THE QUORUM AND READING MINUTES.

Roll call is the first thing after devotion before a deliberative body should proceed to transacting its regular business, and should be always ordered by the presiding officer and called by the recording officer, at once, unless the assembly interfere and order otherwise for the time.

A quorum is a number in a deliberative body to transact business or compel the attendance of absentees. The question of quorum may be fixed, as it often is in parliaments, Legislatures, etc., and often in Boards, but in Baptist assemblies it is not fixed further than to say that the quorum is a majority of the members present. The question of quorum is not raised in Baptist churches, the number assembling, on the time set by the church may transact business legally and no one has the right to complain if he was not present.

READING THE MINUTES OR JOURNAL.

This follows roll call when the quorum has been settled and should be performed every morning upon opening the session and the minutes should be passed upon by the body and corrected if need be.

CIRCULAR LETTER.

TO THE CHURCHES COMPOSING THE FRIENDSHIP ASSOCIATION:

Loving Brethren: Having gone through the business of our meeting, we now address you a short epistle upon the Christian Warfare. This war may be traced in its incipient stages to the first moving of the spirit upon the mind of the sinner, and as conviction increases the war also increases. And the opinion that they can do something themselves to better their condition, with a feeling of pride, and shame is the great barrier to their conversion, and many like the Israleites of old, after leaving Egyptian Bondage, and traveling only three days journey into the wilderness, began to dispair and long for the flesh pots of Egypt, and even for the leeks and garlick; and how many in our day, do return to a servitude of sin, and bondage to the world, and satan? But the sinner having traveled, perhaps forty days in the wilderness, in sore conflict with the enemy, but having obtained a hope, and enlisted in the war, Satan having lost a subject, doubles all his forces to harrass and destroy the young soldier of the cross, and in this stage of the Christians life, not having learned the wars of Canaan, they are often brought low and kept back from duty, and often to doubt the reality of their conviction. But having overcome these temptations and united with the people of God, they are then prepared, and armed for the war, and as this war is not carnal, but spiritual, the weapons also must be spiritual, and they are mighty says the apostle, through God, to the pulling down of strongholds. Truth must be had as a guide, righteousness as a breastplate, and the feet shod with peace, and above all, have the shield of Faith, by which you are to parry, or quench the fiery darts of the wicked, take also the helmed of salvation, and the sword of the Spirit, *the word of God*, and being thus armed, be ready at all times to face the enemy. But mind you, your armor is for defence, and therefore the christian should never through pride, or vain glory, challenge the enemy. Peter the disciple done that, and see the consequences, he denied his

Lord in the presence of a wicked world, who were thirsting for hi life, crying *crucify him! crucify him!* Let this then. dear christiar be a warning to you, least as Peter did, you should also deny you Savior, in companies of the wicked, and before the world, and remember the carnal mind is not changed, and it is through the overture of the mind that access can be had for Satan to tempt the child o God. Seeing, hearing, feeling, tasting, and smelling—any pleasurable feelings the mind can enjoy, comes through some one, or more o the five senses; so also is every feeling of disgust or displeasure Many persons after conversion flatter themselves that the war is over the battle fought and won, they see a clear and cloudless sky, no even dreaming of a tempest close at hand. But remember the lanc of Canaan was promised Israel, but they had to fight and conquer to obtain possession of it. and not only so, but they had perpetual wa to keep possession of it; and you notice there were nations left to prove them, to teach them how to fight, those that had not learned all the wars of Canaan. Namely five lords of the Philistians, corresponding to the five senses of the body, and there were three othe nations also to prove them, the most formidable of all the Cananites. the Sidonian's, and the Levites. These may correspond to the three great sources of evil, spoken of by the apostle John—the lusts of the flesh, the lusts of the eye, and the pride of life. These were left to prove Israel, to know whether they would keep the commandments of God, or not. So are our enemies, they are to prove us, and the most formidable are the three above named, or you may have it, the world, the flesh, and Satan.—The lusts of the flesh, and of the eye, with the pride of life, are truly formidable to the christian; and the christian should never be off his guard, for at every indulgence, or unguarded moment, you may be led astray before you are aware; the lusts of the flesh, or of the eye, or the pride of life, may assail you, and you may be drawn into the snares of vice and folly. And remember,

"Pride, accursed pride, that sin by God abhorred,
Do what we will it haunts us still, and keeps us from the Lord;
This moment, while I write, I feel its power within,
My heart it draws, to seek applause, and mixes all with sin."

No doubt the desire of every christian is to do the will of God.—But the nations were left to prove Israel naturally, are to prove us spiritually, and in some of their various forms are forever haunting the christian, and therefore it is like the wars of Canaan, an unceasing warefare. The good that we would do we do not, and that we would not do, that we do. So then, with the mind the christian serves the law of God, but with the flesh the law of sin. Here then, we can see the great conflict, or warfare in which every christian is engaged, and we hear the apostle saying he had besought the Lord for these things to be removed. But the answer was, My grace is sufficient for thee, and the war had still to go on, and the enemy though often put to flight, yet complete victory never can be obtained while flesh remains. Then christian, you should see to it, be ever ready for the conflict, keep your armor bright and firm upon the watch tower, guard every avenue of the soul, for your enemy as a roaring lion, is roving about seeking whom he may devour, and will try you once and again, and always at the least guarded point. It was thus that Satan tempted our mother Eve in the garden, the language of the serpent at once excited her desires. No doubt to confirm the deception, the serpent would suggest that it was eating that fruit, that enabled him to converse with her. O! what a bait was here offered to that sinless soul! The fruit doubtless had a pleasant scent. The lust of the flesh and of the eye, with the pride of life, all assailed her. No wonder she fell beguiled by the serpent, or Satan, who, we are informed, had the boldness to tempt our Lord by offering him all the kingdoms of the world if he would fall down and worship him. And to resist the enemy successfully, every avenue of the soul must be guarded with diligence, as apart from the five senses of the body, no temptation can assail the christian.

And for our encouragement, we are told to consider him that had endured such contradictions of sinners against himself; least you be worried and faint in your minds, you should call to remembrance the former days, in which after you were illuminated you endured a great fight of affliction, while you were made a gazing stock by reproaches and afflictions, and partly while you become companions of them that were so used. Cast not therefore, away your confidence, for it hath great recompense of reward. And you have great need of the grace of patience, that after you have served the Lord, and finished your trials here, you may receive the promises; and forget not the exhortation which saith unto you, as unto children, my son despise not thou the chastening of the Lord, nor faint under his rebuke, for whom the Lord loveth he chasteneth, and scourgeth every child that he receiveth. And remember, if you are without chastisement whereof all christians are partakers, then are you bastards and not sons. Here is encouragement, dear christian, ponder over your past experience, remember the wormwood, and the gall, keep them still in remembrance with an humble reliance upon God, and he will give you a well grounded hope. Resist the devil and he will flee from you, and in all forget not to pray. The poet says that,

"Satan trembles when he sees, the humblest saint upon his knees." And Bunyan in his Christian, on one occasion found his armor fail, even his sword that had so lately put Apollion to flight, was laid aside, and he betook himself to all prayer, the only channel through which God has ever promised deliverance to man.

A few words to young converts. You have past through the fire of conviction for sin, in which your trials have been many and great, but you have been delivered, your feet taken out of the mire and clay and placed upon a rock, and think it not strange that Satan should attack you somewhat differently from what he has heretofore done. He will suggest to you that all is delusion or deception, or indeed it may be hypocrisy, and if you were a christian you would know it, and not be harrassed with doubts as you are, with many more such doubts as these and shame perhaps will give you many a crimsoned cheek, and tell you not to expose yourself before the world as you do,

Nay, shame is bold enough to try to keep you from the church, and pride will represent to your mind that it is degrading for a person of your standing to be amongst those groaning and whining old fogies, you never can enjoy yourself, nor the company of your equals; you have nothing to tell the church, and you would hate not to be received. A christian knows it, and can tell how the Lord met with them by the way, and spoke peace to their troubled mind. But all is dark with you. the time has past when you might have got religion, but now alas! too late.

These are some of the trials the young Christian often has to meet with, and by which their advance in the divine life is much retarded. But the aged Christian, who has breasted the storm for many years, and is still marching on to victory, can look on calm and tranquil—can meet the conflict with becoming fortitude; and while the young Christians are badly beset with trials and temptations on every hand; and although their own may be very great, yet they have learned by long experience, that it is through much tribulation and patience they are to inherit the promises. And we are authorized to say in the language of Job, That the righteous shall hold on his way, and he that hath clean hands shall be stronger and stronger. And though often cast down, bruised and mangled by the fall, yet the assurance of victory is a sufficient stimulant to the war-worn soldier of the Cross, who at the end of his pilgrimage, will be hailed with "well done good and faithful servant, enter thou into the joys of thy Lord." Written by JAMES WHITAKER, SEN.

MESSENGERS.

MESSENGERS FROM THE CHURCHES FROM 1876 TO 1890.

1876—A. Ammons, J. M. Thomasson, S. J. Freeman, J. S. Tabor, M. Ghormley, W. C. Morgan, G. W. Hooper, William Carpenter, J. M. Smiley, I. T. S. Sherrill, W. H. Cathey, L. L. Thomasson, J. P. Grant, M. DeHart, J. S. Smiley, Young Ammons, B. L. Morgan, W.

D. Crisp, T. H. Cody, John Hyde, David Welch, W. F. Whiteside, J. H. M. Crisp, James Whitaker, R. W. Adams, R. M. Roberts, J. B. Hyde, W. B. Cole, A. J. Parris, T. B. Chambers, E. N. Bumgarner, H. Durham, J. R. Bradshaw, Jasper Truitt, Armstrong Cornsilk, and Jacob Che ah.

1877—A. Ammons, J. R. Edwards, J. M. Welch, J. M. Thomasson, James Dicke Geeska, Armstrong Cornsilk, W. C. Morgan, G. W. Hooper, J. Carringer, H. P. Hyde, J. M. Davis, William Carpenter, C. George, T. A. Carpenter, J. M. Smiley, James Salts, W. H. Cathey, J. M. Earls, J. P. Panther, J. S. Smiley, N. J. Howard, Henry Ramsey, Andrew Watkins, A. Wiggins, E. N. Bumgarner, James Beard, Young Ammons, William Mashburn, M. Bradshaw, T. Y. Ammons, R. M. Roberts, B. J. Delozier, John Hyde, W. F. Whiteside, J. Crisp, P. G. Green, W. D. Crisp, J. L. Crisp, D. A. Taylor, S. A. Crisp, M. A. Crisp, W. Phillips, James Whitaker, R. W. Adams, H. P. Adams, Allen Freeman, J. P Edwards, A. V. Calhoun and Clingman Sawyer.

1878—A. Ammons, J. R. Edwards, C. M. Green, W. C. Morgan, T. A. Carpenter, J. M. Davis, G. W. Hooper, F. M. Morgan, H. A. Cunningham, J. H. M. Whiteside, T. B. Chambers, W. B. Cole, D. Whiteside, A. Wiggins, James Beard, B. L. Morgan, Y. Ammons, James Proctor, J. M. Welch, P. G. Green, J. L. Crisp, W. D. Crisp, H. W. Crisp, W. Phillips, David Adams, R. A. Bradley, B. F. Adams, James Whitaker, R W. Adams, Daniel McCoy, W. L. Welch, A. V Calhoun.

1879—A. Ammons, J. R. Edwards, A. H. Welch, S. J. Freeman, H. M. McHan, C. M. Green, W. C. Morgan, G. W. Hooper, William Pruitt, Van Marcus, Sidney Rose, T. A. Carpenter, William Carpenter, T. C. Buchanan, J. J. Monteith, J. L. Woody, W. B. Cole, J. P. Panther, J. M. Smiley, S. D. Davis, L. L. Thomasson, M. DeHart, J. A. Buchanan, H. A Cunningham, J. M. Earls, D. Whiteside, J Whiteside, J. C. Melton, E. N. Bumgarner, A. W. Parris, Young Ammons, B. L. Morgan, J. A. Ammons, T. Y. Ammons, J. L. Hogue, J. A. Welch, W. A. Marcus, R. H. Crisp, Joseph Whiteside, P. G. Green, Joel L. Crisp, W. D. Crisp, T. H. Cody, H. W. Crisp, Wiley Phillips, James Whitaker, R. W. Adams, Allen Freeman, J. W. Truitt, W. A.

Dorsey, P. Jenkins, Ah-qua-ta-kih, Armstrong Cornsilk and Richard Wright.

1880—J. W. Breenloor, S. J. Freeman, J. M. Welch, W. C. Morgan, G. W. Hooper, T. S. Carpenter, William Carpenter, William Pruitt, H. P. Hyde, J. W. Holland, J. P. Panther, L. L. Thomasson, J. S. Gibby, L. T. Green, H. A. Cunningham, J. A. Buchanan, J. M. R. Smiley, J. A. Thomasson, J. B. Hoyle, T. B. Chambers, J. C. Monteith, A. J. Monteith, J. R. Buchanan, J. M. Smiley, Davis Whiteside, J. Whiteside, Wm. Kirkland, F. P. Hutchins, I. T. S. Sherrill, Jas Beard, E. N. Bumgarner, J. M. Cline, Y. Ammons, B. L. Morgan, J L. Hogue, H. Marcus, T. Y. Ammons, A. J. Ammons, T. J. Calhoun, J. W. Crisp. H. D. Proctor, Nathan Pilkaton, W. F. Whiteside, P. A. Calhoun, P. G. Green, Joel L. Crisp, W. D. Crisp, S. M. Edwards, D. A. Taylor, A. M. Edwards, L. A. Bradley, Jasper Truitt, J. P. Edwards, W. A. Dorsey, John Jenkins, Allen Farmer, P. Jenkins, M. D. Sawyer, Wm. Welch, R. Wright, Jacob Cheer, H. Millsaps, D. Williams.

1881—J. R. Edwards, A. H. Welch, J. M. Collins, William Carpenter, J. A. Hyde, William Pruitt, G. W. Oar, M. DeHart, M. S. Davis, H. A. Cunningham, J. A. Buchanan, A. W. Davis, Noah Birchfield, P. H. Mason, J. M. Earls, S. D. Davis, James Salts, W. B. Cole, A. J. Monteith, J. R. Buchanan, J. M. Smiley, D. S. Colley, Henry Franklin, E. N. J. Whiteside, A. Wiggins, I. T. S. Sherrill, J. P. Panther, E. N. Bumgarner, A. J. Parris, J. R. Bradshaw, B. L. Morgan, J. F. Hogue, D. Pendley, A. L. Weatherman, Richard Wright, P. G. Green, Joel L. Crisp, W. D. Crisp, A. M. Edwards, T. J. Calhoun, P. A Calhoun, J. P. Edwards, F. H. Calhoun, M. S. Sherrill, Wilson Carpenter, T. B. Hyde, T. J. George, D. J. Rogers, S. J. Freeman, J. W. Breedlove, R. H. Freeman, T. S. DeHart, J. A. Ammons, T. L. Wikle, L. M. Medlin and James Proctor.

1882—J. R. Edwards, M. L. Ammons, A. L. McHan, W. C. Morgan, G. W. Hooper, J. E. Morgan, J. W. Holland, Wm. Carpenter, Wm. Pruitt, L. A. Crisp, G. W. Ore, H. P. Hyde, W. S. Thomasson, H. A. Cunningham. L. L. Thomasson, M. DeHart, H. Ramsey, B. L.

Davis, J. M. Earles, James Salts, J. B. Hoyle, J. C. Monteith, E. C. Monteith, J. M. Smiley, A. Wiggins, E. N. Bumgarner, A. W. Parris, John Kimsey, Y Ammons, J. L. Hogue, D. Marcus, F. M. Morgan, A. L. Weatherman, P. G. Green, W. D. Crisp, M. A. Crisp, S. M. Edwards, Joel L. Crisp, D. A. Taylor, J. P. Edwards, I. C. Brooks, John Jenkins, W. L. Welch, P. C. Sawyer, John B. Cable, P. A. Calhoun, W. A. Marcus, J. B. Carringer, W. M. Taylor, Hampton Millsaps, Armstrong Cornsilk, Ah-qua-tee-gi, Jacob Orter, Ute Sherrill, S. L. Carpenter, T. J. Ammons, T. B. Hyde. M. S. Sherrill, J. S. Woodard, S. J. Freeman, John W. Breedlove, James Clampitt, T. N. Freeman, J. L. Proctor, J. D. Proctor, James Proctor, J. R. Bradshaw, B. J. Welch, John Grant, A. L. Adams, T. J. Calhoun, R. A. Crisp, A. J. Willocks, L. M. Medlin, J. C. Hall, E. Wilson and J. F. Hall.

1883—J. R. Edwards, H. M. McHan, M. L. Ammons, Arquetake, L. M. Medlin, J. C. Hall, J. R. Cook, James Russell, Carson Holloway, T. J. Ammons, T. B. Hyde, J. P. Panther, J. M. Earls, E. P. Gibson, J. A. Buchanan, Davis Whiteside, L. L. Thomasson, H. A. Cunningham, J. M. Welch, T. J. Calhoun, C. T. Calhoun, A. J. Willocks, F. H. Calhoun, John C. Calhoun, T. W. Calhoun, W. I. Calhoun, E. C. Monteith, J. B. Hoyle, W. B. Cole, A. J. Parris, S. M. Crawford, J. M. Parris, S. W. Monteith, A. J. Monteith, H. L. Potts, T. S. Monteith, S. A. Monteith, W. R. Monteith, W. M. Anthony, J. B. Hoyle, J. C. Sorrells, D. S. Colley, John Wiggins, J. M. Cline, J. B. Beard, A. W. Parris, E. N. Bumgarner, J. S. Woodard, J. A. Ammons, J. W. Breedlove, D. Davis, J. C. Clampitt, T. N. Freeman, R. T. Cunningham, I. D. Proctor, W. M. Welch, G. W. Welch, James Proctor, J. L. Hogue, D. W. Hogue, James Welch, D. Marcus, John Marcus, J. A. Ammons, L. Medlin, F. M. Morgan, P. G. Green, W. D Crisp, Joel L. Crisp, E. L. Crisp, W. J. Brooks, J. P. Edwards, W. L. Welch, J. C. Edwards, J. H. M. Crisp, John B. Cable, G. W. Crisp, W. A. Marcus, James M. Hyde, J. M. Rickman, Hampton Millsaps, Vance Grant, W. M. Taylor, John P. Grant, J. B. Fuller, W. S. P. Roberts, Wm. Green, J. M. Smiley, J. S. Smiley, J. A. Franks, J. D. Jenkins, N. J. Howard, J. H. Sitton and John Woody.

1884.—J. R. Edwards, A. H. Welch, H. M. McHan, A. L. McHan, William McHan, Armstrong Cornsilk, Obediah Lan-tah, L. Medlin, L. M. Medlin, William Carpenter, T. A. Carpenter, Thomas Rogers, D. J. Rogers, T. B. Hyde, H. P. Hyde, Miller Davis, J. S. Smiley, J. M. Earls, H. Cunningham, L. L. Thomasson, Z. V. Welch, J. A. Buchanan, T. J. Davis, J. S. Gibby, J. M. Smiley, J. M. Welch, D. K. Collins, N. J. Howard, J. H. Sitton, James Kirkland, C. I. Calhoun, A. V. Calhoun, A. J. Willocks. J. H. Sentell, E. C. Monteith, J. C. Monteith, A. C. Hemphill, D. S. Colley, J. C. Melton, A. Wiggins, J. P. Panther, A. W. Parris, J. B. Beard, W. M. Shuler, J. M. Cline, J. S. Woodard, J. A. Ammons, S. J. Freeman, T. N. Freeman, J. W. Breedlove, L. C. Smith, W. L. Proctor, A. M. Grant, A. J. Jones, John Higdon, H. J. Hogue. D. C. Pendley, F. M. Morgan, P. G. Green, W. D. Crisp, J. L. Crisp, A. H. Walker, W. G. Cable, D. A. Taylor, A. M. Edwards, A. L. Adams, C. F. Sawyer, W. D. Sawyer, J. A. Holder, W. L. Welch, Phillip Jenkins, James Woodard, Hampton Millsaps, W. M. Taylor, J. E. Morgan, P. H. Mason, W. C. Hamrick, W. M. Brendle, E. P. Gibson, A. A. Justice and Samuel Ramsey.

1885—J. R. Edwards, L. M. Medlin, J. C. Hall, H. B. Cook, L. Medlin, W. O. Morgan, J. A. Hyde, George Crisp, William Pruitt, Carson Halloway, John Rogers, J. S. Smiley, J. M. Earls, W. A. Cunningham, L. L. Thomasson, Martin DeHart, D. Whiteside, H. H. Hyde, J. A. Franks, J. M. Earls, J. C. Sorrells T. M. Buchanan, Charles Jenkins, J. P. Panther, C. I. Calhoun, J. H. Sentell, W. A. Dorsey, W. I. Calhoun, Z. V. Calhoun, William Nichols, M. V. York, J. C. Crisp. D. S. Colley, J. R. Bradshaw, B. J. Welch, A. W. Parris, J. B. Beard, William Green, A. J. Green, J. A. Ammons, A. A. Wall, J. N. Truitt, J. L. Hogue, J. A. Ammons, John Marcus. N. M. Pilkaton, T. Y. Ammons, P. G. Green, W. D. Crisp, D. A. Taylor, S M. Edwards, A. M. Edwards, Jenkins, A. L. Adams, C. F. Sawyer, Isaac Elliott, W. L. Welch, S. L. Cable, W. D. Sawyer, J. G. Brooks, J. W. Crisp, G. W. Crisp, I. C. Brooks, W. T. Crisp, J. H. M. Crisp, R. H. Crisp, A. A. Justice, W. M. Taylor, Z V. Gunter, John Gibson, W. I. McClure, J. E

Morgan, A. J. Parris, W. B. Cole, E. C. Monteith, G. B. Payne and S. D. Payne.

1886—Armstrong Cornsilk, Jake Cheoah, Tar-que-tee, Lan-tah, L. L. Medlin, H. B. Cook, Lewis Medlin, W. C. Morgan, William Pruitt, G. W. Hooper, G. W. Orr, H. P. Hyde, J. S. Smiley, J. M. Earls, H. A. Cunningham, L. L. Thomasson, J. Buchanan, M. DeHart, N. J. Heward, John Gibson, John Lester, J. U. Whiteside, D. Whiteside, J. J. Bowers, A. Wiggins, J. R Bradshaw, James Proctor, J. H. Queen, J. A. Keenan, W. H. Clark, J. B. Beard, J. S. Woodard, J. W. Breedlove, D. Gufly, W. L. Proctor, D. E. Marcus, J. W. Bradshaw, T. Y. Ammons, J L. Hogue, H. J. Hogue, W. B. Cole, A. J. Parris, E. C. Monteith, M. A. Crisp. W. D. Crisp, Bartley Orr, C. F. Sawyer, W. D. Sawyer, J. P. Panther, C. I. Calhoun, R. H. Crisp, W. H. Marcus, J. H. Sentell, I. C. Brooks, A. J. Willocks, T. S. Calhoun, J. S. Panther, A. A. Justice, B. W. Justice, W. P. Denton, G. B. Payne, J. C. Gunter.

1887—L. M. Medlin, H. M. Cook, J. C. Holloway, J. M. Earls, J. S. Smiley. J. A. Buchanan, L. L. Thomasson, T. Jeffie Davis, S. B. Gibson, J. P. Gibson, W. H. Davis, T. Buchanan, Charles Jenkins, N. F. Snider, J. A. Eranks, J. M. Welch, John Gibson, D. Whiteside, A. Wiggins J. R. Buchanan, J. A. Keenan, William Shuler, David Franklin, J. K. Clark, E. N. Bumgarner, A. W. Parris, T. D. Watson, S. G. Shuler, John Kimsey, J. S. Woodard, J. A. Ammons, J. C. Clampitt, J. T. Cunningham, J. M. Smiley, J. A. Cathey, W. D. Crisp, J. H. Sentell, Thomas Calhoun, A. A. Justice, W. P. Denton, W. H. Queen, H. K. Gass.

1888—E. P. Gibson, Tah-quittee-hee, Jacob Cheer. L. M. Medlin, P. A. Cable, H. M. Cook, J. M. Medlin, M. M. Laney, L. Medlin, William Pruitt, G. W. Hooper, J. J. Colvard, Samuel Jordan, J. M. Davis, W. M. Taylor, J. S. Hyde, T. J. Ammons, J. S. Smiley, J. M. Earls, H. A. Cunningham, M. DeHart, W. H. Davis, J. U. Whiteside, J. S. Gibby, S. B. Gibson, Henry Ramsey, G. H. Church, J. M. Welch, J. A. Franks, T. M. Crawford, J. S. Elmore. John Thomas, J. P. Panther, W. R. Monteith, John Hyde, C. I. Calhoun, T. J. Calhoun, John

Jenkins, James Woodard, A. V. Calhoun, A. C. Hoffman, G. B. Payne, W. B. Cole, E. C. Monteith, J. M. Hyde, D. Whiteside, E. N. J. Whiteside, J. H. Queen, A. W. Parris, J. F. A. Keenan, J. A. Ammons, T. N. Freeman, W. H. Queen, H. K. Gass, Allen Beck, J. A. Cathey, S. Hogue, T. Y. Ammons, D. E. Marcus, H. Hogue, J. Marcus, J. W. Welch, M. A Crisp. D. A. Taylor, S. M. Edwards, A. H. Walker, L. C. Smith, J. C. Edwards, W. D. Crisp, W. M. Barnes,

Wm. Jenkins, F. M. Carringer, W. A. Marcus, C. F. Sawyer, P. C. Brooks, S. L. Cable, W. J. Welch, R. H. Crisp, M. Rogers, J. W. Crisp, J. M. Crisp, A. J. Willocks, A. A. Justice, S. T. Ramsey, J. R. Anderson and J. L. Smith.

1889—J. M. Collins, A. L. McHan, J. R. Kimzey, T. D. Watson, A. P. Childers, Adam Conseen, William Pruitt, J. M. Smiley, J. S. Smiley, T. S. DeHart, W. H. Davis, L. Frisbee, J. A. Buchanan, J. A. Franks, E. C. Monteith, J. C. Calhoun, D. S. Colley, A. Wiggins, J. H. Queen, J. B. Beard, A. W. Parris, H. K. Gass, J. S. Woodard, J. W. Breedlove, J. C. Clampett, J. P. Panther, J. P. Grant, L. M. Medlin, T. Y. Ammons, W. D. Crisp, A. A, Justice, W. P. Denton, H J. Beck. J. M. Mathis, J. S. Conner, W. H. Queen, S. L. Beck, W. E. Queen, A. L. Adams, W. B. Gibson, D. K. Blanton, S. P. Harwood and J. W. Rogers.

1890—G. L. Tabor, A. W. Wall, A. L. McHan, Andrew Orter, Adam Conseen, T. D. Watson, J. K. Kimsey, J. A. Childers, G. H. Church, J. M. Welch, J. A. Franks, J. S. Elmore, T. M. Crawford, M. J. Beek, Robert Moody, J. M. Davis, T. J. Ammons, T. L. Rogers, Jno. S. Smiley, J. M. Smiley, J. M. Earls, T. S. DeHart, H. A. Cunningham, W. L. Panther, J. P. Gibson, W. H. Davis, J. A. Buchanan, F. P. Hutchins, W. R. Monteith, John Gibson, B. F. Fowler, T. J. Calhoun, A. V. Calhoun, John Jenkins, I. B. Elliott, W. B. Cole, J. C. Monteith, A. C. Hoyle, John Lester, A. J. Monteith, E. C. Monteith, T. W. Calhoun, P. A. J. B. Styles, J. C. Calhoun, D. Whiteside, W. S. Whiteside, A. Wiggins, D. S. Colley, Joseph Colley, H. K. Gass, John Wiggins, W. H. Clark, J. H. Queen, H. J. Beck, W. H.

Queen, W. E. Queen, J. H. Beck, I. V. Hooper, J. S. Woodard, J. A. Ammons, J. C. Clampett, H. M. DeHart, T. L. Wikle, R. T. Cunningham, H. H. Hyde, J. P. Grant, G. W. Grant, C. M. Brendle, J. R. Edwards, Calvin Hunnicutt, L. M. Medlin, T. Y. Ammons, N. M. Pilkaton, J. M. Medlin, J. W. Welch, A. B. Thomas, M. A. Crisp, A. H. Walker, S. M. Edwards, J. R. Stratton, P. P. Harwood, Sen., J. P. Panther, I. C. Brooks, M. Rogers, John Crisp, A. J. Willocks, A. A. Justice, B. W. Justice, J. W. Justice, Joseph Morgan, H. C. Burnett, John Anderson. J. B. Fuller, A. J. Green, W. C. Hamrick and S. M. Evans.

THE END.

www.ingramcontent.com/pod-product-compliance
Lightning Source LLC
Chambersburg PA
CBHW020544270326
41927CB00006B/706

* 9 7 8 3 3 3 7 3 0 2 2 0 7 *